...ins' poems
...oulated by
...oetic proj-

Coleman

...Kavanagh,

...ten taking the form of dra-...his poems springing out of colloquial address and celebrating the ordinary through a use of quotidian bric-a-brac, which he often pits - with positive effect - against larger (but no more important) forces...Comedy is part of his poetics, and what I especially like in his work is its swiftness of wit, its tone of buoyant contrarianism and jubilant disappointment", **Eamon Grennan**, *The Irish Times*

"It is a profound compliment to the quality of Kevin's writing that you can disagree with the content and yet find yourself still reading on and appreciating the style. You'd have to say that he is one of the lead poets of his generation in Ireland at this stage."
Clare Daly T.D.

"Gil Scott Heron's The Revolution Will Not Be Televised as re-told by Victor Meldrew".
Phil Brown, *Eyewear*

"Fluent and often as laugh-out-loud funny as Paul Howard's Ross O'Carroll-Kelly."
John McAuliffe, *The Irish Times*

"Higgins is a genius, because he does something only great poets do: he writes with a voice that is entirely his own, in a style he has invented, about themes and concerns that now are instantly recognisable as his terrain." **Todd Swift**

"Ireland's sharpest satirist my arse." **Fergus Finlay**

"Ireland's best political poet" **Mike Jenkins**, former editor of *Poetry Wales*

"Brilliant satire." **Peter Tatchell**

"Kevin Higgins writes political poetry of the highest order, telling truth to power with Swiftian savagery and satirical humour, dissecting and denouncing political doublespeak, pretension and hypocrisy." **Mike Quille**, *Culture Matters*

salmonpoetry

Publishing Irish & International
Poetry Since 1981

Song of Songs 2.0

New & Selected Poems

KEVIN HIGGINS

Published in 2017 by
Salmon Poetry
Cliffs of Moher, County Clare, Ireland
Website: www.salmonpoetry.com
Email: info@salmonpoetry.com

ISBN 978-1-910669-84-6

COVER ARTWORK: *Mark Jameson*
COVER DESIGN & TYPESETTING: *Siobhán Hutson*
Printed in Ireland by Sprint Print

Salmon Poetry gratefully acknowledges the support of
The Arts Council / An Chomhairle Ealaoín

for Susan Millar DuMars, Darrell Kavanagh,
& Mary Higgins (RIP) without whom none of this

Acknowledgments

Acknowledgements are due to the editors of the following publications in which versions of some of the new poems in this selection first appeared: *Poetry Ireland Review, The Café Review* (Portland, Maine, U.S.A) Special Irish Issue, *The Bogman's Cannon, Anomaly Literary Magazine* (U.K.), *Poethead* (Ed. Chris Murray), *Harry's Place* (U.K.), *Penduline Press* (U.S.A.), *Communion Literary Magazine* (Australia), *Eyewear, The Blog* (Ed. Todd Swift), *Socialist Unity* (Ed. Andy Newman), *Scum Gentry — Alternative Arts & Media, Culture Matters* (Ed. Mike Quille), *The Morning Star* (U.K.), *Southword* (Ed. Thomas McCarthy), *The Irish Examiner*, Clare Daly TD's Facebook page, *The Recorder* (U.S.A), *more raw material — work inspired by Alan Sillitoe* (Ed. Neil Fulwood & David Sillitoe), *The Stony Thursday Book* (Ed. Mary O'Donnell), *Poetry & All That Jazz* (Chichester Poetry Festival), *The Pickled Body, The Pileus* (UK), & *Lucifer magazine* (UK), & *Even The Daybreak — 35 Years of Salmon Poetry* (Ed. Jessie Lendennie).

'Inappropriate Comparisons' was broadcast on RTE Radio One's *Arena* programme.

This selection also includes poems which previously appeared in the collections *The Boy With No Face* (Salmon, 2005), *Time Gentlemen, Please* (Salmon, 2008), *Frightening New Furniture* (Salmon, 2010), *The Ghost In The Lobby* (Salmon, 2014), *2016 — The Selected Satires of Kevin Higgins* (Nuascéalta, 2016), & *The Minister for Poetry Has Decreed* (Culture Matters, 2016).

Contents

NEW POEMS

Question Asked Me By Young Woman Who Recently Won A Marathon	12
Selfie	13
To Those Who Preferred The Old Kevin	15
My Wishes For You	17
Song of Songs 2.0	18
The Proper Practice of Mindlessness	20
Eat Yourself	21
False Prophet	22
It Was For This	24
Poem In The Manner Of The Late Kevin Higgins	26
Manifesto of The Last International	27
Idealistic Times	28
The Eternal Peace Activist	29
War and Peace	31
The Scissors	32
On A Prodigious Philanthropist's Ghastly Second Death	33
Laddering Tights	35
Streets I'd Not Revisit	37
Of Course They Know It's Christmas	39
The New Rising Will Not Be Available Later On The RTE iPlayer	41
Sympathy For The Sympathetic	44
I Am Pleased To Congratulate On Behalf Of The People of Ireland	45
What They Don't Know Is	47
from Tax	48
Conference Speech	50
Governing Council Statement on Recent Non-standard Measures	52
The So-Called World	54
Pictures of Unfamiliars	55

On The New Parliamentary Rump In The Absence
  of Mandatory Reselection   57
The Sudden Thaw & What It's Doing To You   58
On The Departure From Office Of Barack Obama   59
Surprised By Joy (whatever her name is)   60
Things To Do In Galway Before You Again Decide
  Not To Shoot Yourself   61
Not Red Nor A Rose, No   62
Epithalamium   63
To Whom It Definitely Concerns   64
The Undoing   66
Inappropriate Comparisons   67

SELECTED POEMS

from The Boy With No Face (2005)

To Hell And Back Again   69
By Five o'clock   70
To Certain Lyric Poets   71
I Am Ireland   72
President Robinson Pays Homage To Lord Haw Haw   73
A Postcard from Minneapolis   74
Café Du Journal   75
A Real Galwegian   76
Desperate Weather   77
A Brief History of Those Who Made Their Point
  Politely And Then Went Home   78
Else   79
January   80
Almost Invisible   81
Letter To A Friend About Girls   82
Blackhole   83

from Time Gentlemen, Please (2008)

Foreboding   86
From the future, a postcard home   87
The Couple Upstairs   88
Tuesday   89
My Militant Tendency   90
Conversation with a Former Self   91
Dad   92
Ending Up   93
The Great Depression   95
The Candidate   96
Reasons for doing The John Walker Lindh   97
Firewood   98
Word From The Other Country   99
Shapeless Days Shuffling   100
Retirement   101

from Frightening New Furniture (2010)

St. Stephen's Day, 1977   103
That Was My Country   104
Ourselves Again   105
Without   106
House Guest   107
The Lost Years   108
Days   109
The Country I Dreamt Up While Protesting
    On Shop Street   110
Clear Out   111
Comrades   112
His Hour Come Round At Last   113
Bookshop Romance   114
Midnight Mass   115
Getting Somewhere   116
Together In The Future Tense   117

from The Ghost In The Lobby (2014)

Historically Sensible	119
On Getting Away With It	120
My Inner Conspiracy Theorist	121
Remembering the Nineties	122
Not	123
Them and You	124
God Has Put You On Hold	125
Irish Government Minister Unveils Monument to Victims of Pro-Life Amendment	126
What The Virgin At Knock Would Say If She Could Speak	127
Austerity Mantra	128
Lament For A Latter Day Progressive	129
Autobiography	130
Mouth	131
You Can Take The Man Out Of Eyre Square But You Can't Take The Eyre Square Out Of The Man	132
The Death of Baroness Thatcher	133

from 2016 – The Selected Satires of Kevin Higgins (2016)

Blair's Advice	136
Irish Air: Message from the CEO	138
Irish Liberal Foresees Own Enduring Relevance	141
Renewable Energy: Cora Sherlock's Excellent Suggestion	143
The Islamisation of Birmingham	145

from The Minister for Poetry Has Decreed (2016)

The Art of Political Rhetoric	148
Against Plan to Ruin Revolution Day with Strike	150
Ghost of Health Service Future	152
A Day of Just Yes	154
Exit	156
Afterword by Philip Coleman	159
About Kevin Higgins	166

New Poems

Question Asked Me By Young Woman
Who Recently Won A Marathon

And do you run?
>   From the sound of this
cough, I'm running nowhere
>   except out of time. Since
Mom left to debate the finer points
>   with Lady Gregory and William Joyce
—late of Rutledge Terrace
>   and the Third Reich—up there
in the Cemetery; I'm aware,
>   for the likes of me, more is gone
than is to come.

>   I expect, any year now,
to fall off that ladder
>   I never go up,
to be staring blankly on the path
>   when whoever it is finds me.
Or one morning in the bathtub
>   to clutch hard both my rubber duck
and my anus, as I'm struck
>   by a terror cold as the North Sea.
Then, slack jawed, letting go.
>   Everything. All at once.

Selfie

"At 50, everyone has the face he deserves."
George Orwell

My hair is the grass
on the local five-a-side pitch
at the end of the worst winter
since nineteen forty seven.

My eyebrows, more
than my personal groomer—
the cat— can handle right now.

My eyes are light blue jellyfish
floating in increasingly
opaque sea-water.

The fuzz up my nose,
and in my ears, that patch
of grass the university groundsman
keeps forgetting to cut.

My ears, two elderly uncles
successfully avoiding each other
at opposite ends of a wedding.

My skin, the well-thumbed book
you picked up in a charity shop,
and never got around to finishing.

In their last exam, my lungs
got fifty three per cent,
so won't be going to university
unless I give them to medical science.

My belly is one of those small insults
you get away with
because you've had Champagne,
but should generally keep
itself to itself.

My penis is a vintage car
one only takes out
every so often.

My knees and ankles are machinery
made almost obsolete
by recent developments.

The crack down the gable wall
has moved and is now
within me.

To Those Who Preferred The Old Kevin

I'm sorry the boy who loved
      Nicaraguan peasants
and striking coalminers
      but not himself
is no longer available
      to not take
your advice. Sorry

      I didn't end up walking
the streets in the weather
      with a bin bag,
contents undetermined. Sorry

      I no longer occasionally
sleep in railway stations,
      and don't turn up for work
because I'm too busy forcing
      upon the world
change it doesn't want.

      If the person you're looking for
hadn't so tragically ceased to exist,
      I'd happily send him over
to make your spare room
      his, and use your telephone
without paying for it. Sorry

      I'm no longer
not turning up for the exam,
      or having near death experiences
in the kitchen, Stoke Newington,
      September, 1989,
but never actually
      getting around
to turning on the gas.

Sorry
I'm no longer so thin
      starving kittens
take pity on me.

      Tomorrow I'll send you
a ring of white lilies
      and my sympathy
on the death of who
      the fool I was
made you think you were.

My Wishes For You

That your son at Trinity College
      may graduate
to become a rogue gynaecologist.
      That his brother, the paediatrician,
be suspended without pay.
      That your husband be caught
selling wheelchairs that don't work
      live on national radio. And the day

you discover all of the above, may
      the traffic wardens, every one of them,
be East Galway Gestapo. May you lose
      your winning ticket,
and the gun not go off
      when it's supposed to.

May your reflux be acid
      and your bowel be cranky.
May your water forever be cloudy
      and the pharmacy be shut.
May the funeral parlour
      refuse you,

and the lies you told haunt you
      long after the cat
has made a litter tray of your ashes.

Song of Songs 2.0

after Anonymous 3rd or 2nd Century B.C.

How glorious your feet stuffed into trainers
Oh lavatory attendant's daughter.
The joints of your thighs pop
out like cuckoo clocks;
the work of a drunken assembly line operative
on his last day at the factory.

Your navel is the tiniest china cup
from which I will sup
Carlsberg Special. Your belly is sweet potatoes
gone off in a sack.

Your breasts sway, like the crowd
at a football match
at the end of which
they killed the referee.

Your head is that of a poorman's Lady Jane Grey,
whom the axeman has forgotten.
And the hair on it is red
as the face of a businessman
whose wife came home
much earlier than expected.

Your neck is a gilded iron girder.
Your eyes are two fishtanks
emptied for cleaning.
Your nose is the bend on the Rhine
and sniffs out even the smallest rodent
up a tree somewhere in the Black Forest.

Your stature is that of a great Irish Oak,
upon which even a chainsaw
makes no impression.
And your breasts, of which we must once again speak,
are also like Nixon and Gerald Ford
discussing Watergate in secret.

I will climb up your trunk
and blow your nose for you,
until you sound like the train
from Hertford East arriving early
at Liverpool Street station.

For the roof of your mouth is like
cheap whiskey that makes men
whose livers gave out get up
angry from their graves.

Let us get up early to the canal
by the chemical weapons factory
and see what dies there.
There I will give you my love
and let you unfasten my cassock.

Afterwards, we'll smell like peaches
gone soft and pulpy
from years spent under my bed
waiting especially for you.

The Proper Practice of Mindlessness

after Jon Kabat-Zinn

Consider each of your days a ribboned gift box
which, if opened with curiosity,
will reveal an alarm clock telling you
not to panic. The chair may give way
under your rear each morning,
but your tailbone will welcome
the concrete floor's
valuable contribution to the debate.
When you arrive back late
from a disappointing holiday
in Enfield Wash, and the key snaps in the lock;
you'll realise that outside in the developing
hailstones is where you wanted to be
all along. Breathe
properly and the amphetamines
will just make you calmer.
Focus on the immediately,
if not sooner, and those steroid
tablets, washed down occasionally
with Champagne, will have you talking
nothing but common sense.
Live in the never
and you'll be two whole halves
of the same self,
your Yin and your Yum Yum in perfect
imbalance.

Eat Yourself

after Rosanna Davison

Accessorise yourself with genetically modified eyebrows
Batter yourself in cement mix
Crap yourself beautiful
Dye yourself bright yellow
Eat yourself with a special set of false teeth you ordered
    from the Kama Sutra
Garnish yourself with knotweed
Lick yourself leathery
Moon yourself in the shop window
Numb yourself in a bathtub filled with Dettol
Undo yourself with vodka martinis
Order yourself a copy of yourself from the catalogue

Fillet yourself twice weekly on the chopping board mother gave you
Heal yourself with hydrochloric acid
Inter yourself under the new driveway
Jail yourself in a greenhouse full of false widow spiders grown bitter
Kill yourself by drowning unintentionally in liquidized beetroot
Peel yourself regularly with an onion slicer that takes its issues
    out on people like you
Question yourself harshly with the rustiest breadknife you can find
Roll yourself in the worst lemon meringue money ever changed
    hands for
Starve yourself stupid
Tie yourself to a tree with your grandfather's vast collection
    of leather belts
Vaporise yourself with an improvised atom bomb
Wrap yourself in the compost heap
Exonerate yourself never
Yap yourself skinny
Zip yourself the fuck up

False Prophet

after Kate Tempest

See him, the old fool, his eyebrows plucked out.
Alone in the launderette with his bag of parsnips.
Witness to every terrible idea that rose up in anger
and fell prey to its opposite. *This is communism.*
I think he said. Or was it maybe
Fucking abominable? He's the sort who gets up slowly
from the toilet seat, gripping his zipper
when he discovers it's the Ladies.

Friendless, a bit cross eyed, at night tap dancing
the national anthem. He empties little
bottles of whiskey, has conversations
with the crows. *Every bastard with half an arse
is busy talking up the apocalypse,
while I'm in the bathtub just dreaming
of beating the Queen Mum's head in
with a shovel.* Afternoons he leaves his flat
still with a semi and stains down his front.

He stops to rip down political posters
and sometimes brings home
dogs that belong to other people.
Ice Cream for breakfast. Afternoon tea
in a cup with a beetle floating in it.
Each time celebrating
going to the toilet.
Some days he wakes up thinking
he's Philip Schofield.
Other times imagines he's
Jack 'The Hat' McVitie.
These are the days when
he can be who he wants.

Romanians upstairs.
Farage on the telly. In bed he picks
his toenails with a plastic fork
he got from the kebab shop
the day it shut. He taps his good foot
to anything by Doris Stokes. Says he once had a date
with the widow of Kelvin McKenzie.
All my life I've paid
to watch black women wrestle.
Watching them sweat makes me feel special.

He keeps the finger he lost
in an industrial accident
during Harold Wilson
hidden away under
the kitchen sink
in a box that came
with a Chinese takeaway,
alongside the ring he bought
for a woman whose name
he mostly forgets.

It Was For This

after Stephen Murphy

      That Queen Maeve prepared for battle
by angrily shaving her armpits with a razor
      improvised from north Fermanagh shale.
For this W.B. Yeats took all that
      experimental Viagra, and waited for
the consequences to grow. For this
      Archbishop McQuaid
rolled naked through fields of Lavender.
      For this Maude Gonne let slip
from her womb a future
      Minister for External Affairs,
while loudly denying
      the Holocaust in Irish.
For this Oliver J. Flanagan warned us:
      "where the bees are there is the honey,
and where the Jews are there is the money"
      For this latter day Druids moved
to Ballyvaughan or west Cork,
      and began accepting payment by PayPal.
For this Fiachra of the fashionable whiskers
      took his herbal tincture and sat
letting silence surround him
      for the twenty four hours
his homeopath recommended. For this
      genuine girls all over Ireland
are waiting for your call
      after you stop shouting
at the terrible news. For this
      you paid the phone bill though it left
your bank account burnt
      as a cottage visited once too often
by the black and tans. For this
      on wild Atlantic nights –

the lines down and the cattle crying
        in the fields, you keep trying
to get through – though you're pretty sure
        some of those girls aren't genuinely
girls. For this Eoin O'Duffy
        put all his bulls in the one field
and dreamed of one day
        holding in this hand
Heinrich Himmler's mickey. For this
        Sean O'Casey broke the window
to let the winter in
        and wrote letters backing
the Hitler-Stalin pact. For this
        Dr Maureen Gaffney of Trinity College
went on the radio every Saturday
        to express concern about poverty,
and people phoned in to agree.
        For this the people of Roscommon drank
from their toilets, and threw up
        thankful prayers to the monks
at Glenstal Abbey. For this
        you voted to keep the black babies out
a sensible policy for a cleaner
        Glenamaddy, Hacketstown, Portlaoise...
For this the bus driver didn't stop just now
        when he saw you waving.

All that history
        so you can stumble up the steps,
sweat gushing from your armpits, late
        for that crucial interview; or arrive
at the hospital ten minutes after
        they've switched off the respirator
and folded the sheet white
        over your father's face.
It was all for this.

Poem In The Manner of
The Late Kevin Higgins

"What is most striking is his immense self-regard."

Member of the Socialist Party whose name no one remembers

I am not the walrus, but the sausage
you couldn't be bothered to eat in St. Louis.
I'm the massage lounge at Cleveland Airport
you didn't have the courage to visit.
If I was an article in the New Yorker
I'd mention Leon Trotsky at least
seventeen times and you'd read me
(but not to the end) at a motorway stopover
near Stevenage. I'm General Pinochet
with what appears to be a smiling face.
I'm the man who lives in a broom closet
with no doors and a broom only he can see.
I'm the ashtray it's now illegal to use.
I'm the game-show host
with the terrible green sweater
who years from now will be bundled
into the back of a police car
with an *Aldi* bag over his whitened mullet.
I'm the doctor who called
your recurring bladder infection
the pneumonia of the South.
I'm everyone taken away
in the middle of the night
(or at least before the ice cream arrived)
for writing subversive haiku.
And I'm those who did the taking.

Manifesto of The Last International: Address To The Men and Women of Waterlooville

with a little help from Darrell Kavanagh & Quincy Lehr

Our movement will be henceforth called
Death to Bruce Forsyth. We will abolish all
immigration controls. Burqas
will be mandatory for supporters
of West Ham United and Millwall.
We will re-appoint Lord Reith
(1889-1971) Director-General of the BBC.
There will be compulsory German lessons
for the unemployed. Sexual congress
between residents of Basingstoke
will be prohibited forthwith. The Church
of England and National Coal Board will be merged.
Public schools will be converted into saunas
for unconsenting homosexuals. Local bus services
will be replaced, as of January 2016, with sedan chairs
carried by ex-members of the newly extinguished
Confederation of British Industry.
The smoking of *Slim Panatella* cigars
will be compulsory for school children
from year three onwards. Each workday
will begin with the singing
of the collected works of Gary Glitter.
The capital of England will rotate
triennially between Crawley, Havant and Bordeaux.
The new twenty pound note will bear the mugshot
of the late Unity Mitford with tastefully drawn on
gunshot wound. We will declare war,
first on Tibet, then on ourselves.

Idealistic Times

"It was an exciting time to be young."
Homer Simpson

We were busy taking control of our
cable TV accounts by signing up online,
to avail of the smallest discount in history.
I was upstairs playing with my make-your-own
Mitt Romney set. Wife was in the shed
deciding, in the end, not to have sex
with the boy who used to mow,
among other things, our lawn.
Her brother was under the duvet
breaking his own record
by, in one day, deciding to join neither
the Bolshevik Party nor the Continuity IRA.
My cousin, the footballer, was
not coming on as a substitute
in a match abandoned due to a
waterlogged pitch. Uncle,
the politician, was announcing
he wasn't running
for Parish Council, posting
his No We Can't speech on Youtube
for people everywhere not to listen to.

People like us - who make this
world what it, mostly, is - were busy
not letting the cat in
or accidentally
putting our drivers' licences,
our social security cards, our lives
where we'd never find them again.

The Eternal Peace Activist

after Donovan and Pete Seeger

When the child soldiers came to our village,
I offered them green, red, yellow
lollipops.

I didn't throw grenades at black limousines
carrying Nazi leaders
through Czechoslovakia.

I spent the morning
of the St. Bartholomew's Day
massacre, trying to organise
a group hug.

During the Sack of Constantinople
I was busy writing
a strongly worded statement
against the blood that ran
in the gutters like rain.

Each night I pray
they'll leave it to the United Nations,
Arab League, Warsaw Pact to sort
out amongst themselves.

I asked Genghis Khan
where all the flowers had gone?;
told Chemical Ali about the universal
soldier who, unlike me, really is to blame.

When you showed me room after room
of your relatives' carefully stacked skulls,
I said: the internal affairs
of Democratic Kampuchea
are not my business.

Even if one of those heads
was mine, I'd not lift
a fingernail to keep it attached
to its owner, think the peace talks in Paris
must be given another chance.

When a four foot boy clad in black
bomber jacket shoved a lit kerosene rag,
through my neighbour's letterbox,
I didn't take the easy way out
and familiarize his cranium
with the pavement.

Now, he's six foot eight
and has a gang who go around with him.

War and Peace

When Peace comes,
and War is put away in the museum;
    when Smart Bomb and Kalashnikov
go the way of gramophone, stocks, and
    death by sawing, and there is never again
a cross word between nations;
    when all we see on TV
and internet of the Middle East
    are pictures of people fanatically
seeing the other guy's point of view;
    when the Confederacy of Cats
and Parliament of Mice end
    their centuries old disagreement;
and the rattlesnake is ordered
    by the UN Secretary General
to place his fangs under
    international supervision;

we'll slowly forget its name
    War. Children will think it
something from an old science fiction film.
    There'll be so much Peace,
we'll be busy not knowing what to do with it,
    when, somewhere
we've probably never heard of,
    one guy takes something
the other guy says is his,
    and while we're dozing
on the sofa or forgetting to brush our teeth,
    they'll start bringing
Metternich, Clemenceau, Henry Kissinger,
    and the Intercontinental Ballistic Missile,
back from the dead to teach us again
    the meaning of certain words.

The Scissors

after Yehuda Amichai

Seven inches long with red, plastic handles.
It cut the cord on bales of briquettes, helped them
make good nights the sky was ice and
the wind sarcastic down the chimney.
It trimmed eyebrows; liberated
biographies of Fidel Castro and
the comedian Frankie Boyle, books on
every aspect of human psychology
from Amazon boxes. It pared toenails
of both sexes to bare essentials.
For the child whose mother rented
the flat before them, it once cut stars
from silver paper. Lately, it mostly
sliced through string
on cooked chickens; tore open
bags of cat litter. This evening

she briefly considered planting it
in the base of his neck, like the flag at Iwo Jima,
before he could wake from his nap to repeat
that thing he'd been saying all week,

on balance decided not to; instead
clipped a photograph of them
both from the local paper,
which tomorrow she'll get
framed.

On A Prodigious Philanthropist's Ghastly Second Death

after Bernie Taupin

Goodbye your shiny tracksuits,
though I never saw one unzipped;
they had the grace to hide your bits,
while those around you fawned.
They made you Knight Bachelor -
for charitable services. Then had
your granite headstone
goodness gracious dismantled
and sent to landfill
near Skipton.

And it seems to me you lived
your life *as it happens* loving children,
you got from various hospitals,
in the back of your silver Rolls Royce.
Never knowing when Mary Whitehouse
might give you an award for services
to family friendly TV,
and you'd be forced
to wind the window down
to accept it. And I would
have liked to know you
but I was just a kid.
Your cigar burnt out long before
I ever got to smoke it.

Their jealousy towards you odious.
Not everyone can be a crony of
both Margaret Thatcher and
Cardinal Basil Hume.
The University of Leeds gave you

how's about that, then an honorary
doctorate of law. And pain
was the price they paid.
Even when you died, pundits
whispered behind fists,
when the microphone was safely off,
that Jimmy was found *now then, now then*
with his mitts up a girl's dress.

Goodbye England's shiny tracksuit,
though I never got to look inside you,
from the boy watching
Top of The Pops, Christmas 1976,
who sees you as something more than sexual
more than just our Sir James Wilson Vincent Savile,
Order of the British Empire.

And it seems to me you lived
your life *as it happens* fixing children,
you got from various hospitals,
in the back of your silver Rolls.
Never knowing when Tony Blair
might invite you to dine at Chequers.
I would have liked to know
you but *guys and gals* I was just a kid.
And pain was the price they paid.

Laddering Tights

after Kate Bush

You take it out and show me,
and we roll violently around on the green
Sunday evenings when the rest of the Village
are home planning to kill their wives.
You have a temper, like my lactose intolerance,
my peanut allergy combined.

Bad tummy in the night
I thought I was going to lose
the bean chilli with chocolate and walnuts
you made me, leave my laddering, laddering,
laddering tights
behind on the bathroom floor.

You are Cliff Richard, only crueller.
Totally bald now and the top of my head's
so cold! Let me climb back in your letter box and show you
the things I learned at art school.

It gets dark out here and the street is full of loonies,
all of whom remind me of you.
Without you I whine a lot,
whine a lot, find
the ceiling comes clattering down
covers me in fine white dust,
even when I'm outside,
wailing in your scullery air vent.

You are crueller even
than Sir Edward Heath
to leave me out here singing like this.
Yours the only face I want to see
when I tear off your gimp mask

and show the moves
I learned at the interpretive dance class
you made me take.

I've come home.
And it's fucking cold out here.
Let me in your bathroom window.

Let me grab it, almost
yank it right off and put it
in a toasted rye bread sandwich.

You made me leave my laddering, laddering,
laddering tights
behind on the cruel bathroom floor
and, in the circumstances,
the least you could do
is not leave me here with my howling head
wedged in your bastard cat flap.

Streets I'd Not Revisit

after Charlene

Hey fatso, you laddy, cursing at the wife,
someone's malcontented daddy,
shaking a hedge clippers at your life.
No doubt you spank
yourself over the things you think I do.
I wish someone had lifted me by my lapels
like I'm going to grab you
by yours.

I've been down Grope Lane and Hackney Wick
and anywhere there weren't electronic
gates to keep me out. I've more than once
helped the wrong type of woman
break her mother's one
and only couch.

I've sold commie newspapers door to door
on the twentieth floor
of blocks since demolished;
painted slogans I now know to be lies
on buildings all around Kensal Rise.
I've a map somewhere of *Workers' Paradise*,
full of streets I'd not revisit.

I've twitched like Andreas Baader
hoping to make it through airport
security at Frankfurt Main, as once again I boarded
the bus with a travel card
that was out of date. I've drank cans
of *Kestrels* down the Green Man
and in the morning couldn't
find a pulse.

I've known weeks when Sunday lunch
was a sausage roll I had to assemble myself;
slurped tea in a condemned mug
straight from the microwave,
with bits floating in it that were likely
still alive.

I've done DIY dentistry
on every one of my top front teeth,
have the incomplete smile to prove it.
I've watched Class War anarchists
throw fire extinguishers at cops,
while you were upstairs trying on
your latest tank top.

I've been to *Paradise*,
mate, and don't plan a return visit. So, belt
up and do as she says.

Of Course They Know It's Christmas

after Midge Ure & Bob Geldof

It's Christmastime; and there's every reason to be afraid
At Christmastime, we let the light love us and we banish shame
Down our streets of plenty we can spread the smirk of money
Throw your arms around a former bass guitarist
Whose name you think is Chris at Christmastime

But ping your pennies at the other ones
In the long line outside the foodbank
As you drive loudly past
In your silver BMW
Because it's better than paying tax

At Christmastime
It gets hard, though not as hard as it used to, when you're having fun
With a reupholstered former model who claims to be a cousin
Of General Pinochet's personal physician
There's a world outside your triple-gazed PVC window
And it's a world of fear and hate
Where the only water flowing is the bitter sting
Of an accountant from Penge
Peeing on rough sleepers
Because his train is late again

We could've kept our enormous
Mouths shut, or had the good taste
To be found dead in suspicious
Circumstances at least a decade ago
Instead we offer
A bunch of rock stars who'd be forgotten
If it wasn't for this old song

And the alarms that go off there
Are the clanging chimes of private property

Well tonight thank Lucifer it's them instead of Bono
And there will be ice in sleeping bags this Christmastime
The greatest gift they'll get this year is death
Remind them that it's Christmastime
In case they missed the ads

"The New Rising Will Not Be Available Later On The RTE iPlayer"

after Gil Scott Heron

There will be no avoiding it, gobshite.
You will not be able to log on, click like and see both sides.
It will interrupt your plans for a gap year in Thailand,
or to skip out for a wank during the new Guinness ad.
The new rising will not be available later on the RTE iPlayer.

Because it will not be suitable for children
or county councillors of diminutive stature who might find it
by accident on the internet while trying to hire
a hitwoman or a dominatrix in the greater Ballyseedy area,
or open an offshore account on the Aran Islands.

The new rising will not be available later on the RTE iPlayer.
Will not be presented by Joe Duffy
in four parts with every possible intrusion
from people trying to sell you bits of Allied Irish Bank
or *butter that's more spreadable than Ebola*.
The new rising will not show you pornographic clips
of Micheál Martin blowing the biggest tin whistle
in recent Irish history and leading a charge by Eamon
Dunphy, and all the assembled wise men of Aosdána
on the kitchens of the Shelbourne Hotel.

It will not be available later on the RTE iPlayer
or be brought to you by the Abbey Theatre
not Waking The Nation. It will not feature
guest appearances from Princess Grace of Monaco,
Graham Norton, and Bono's old sunglasses.
The new rising will not give your Danny Healy Rae
blow up doll sex appeal. It will have no advice
on how to reduce the size of your moobs

overnight in the greater Cootehill
area by just dialling this number.
It will not try to sell you
travel insurance every time you buy
a bus ticket to anywhere in Sligo.

There will be no pictures of you, Mary Kennedy, and Daithi
Ó Sé pushing shopping trolleys around Supervalu
in aid of Children In Need, or trying to smuggle the body
of Ann Lovett onto a flight to Medjugorje
in aid of CURA. The new rising
will not be available later on the RTE iPlayer.
Harry McGee's haircut will not be able
to predict the result by midday the following day
based on reports in now from 43 constituencies.
And it will not be available later on the RTE iPlayer.

There will be no pictures of well ironed Garda uniforms
dangling known subversives out high windows
in strict accordance with the law.
There will be no pictures of Joan
Burton and Katherine Zappone being run out of Jobstown
in the extreme discomfort of cars paid for by you,
pretending they're rushing off to
Repeal the 8th Amendment.

Whether or not Louis Walsh dyes his
pubes will no longer be relevant. Nobody
will care if Paul finally gets to screw
everyone on Fair City, including
himself, because the small people
will be in the street turning on the sunshine.
And this will not be available later on the RTE iPlayer.

To assist the re-education of those
who insist on just watching it on TV,
the Angelus immediately before the Six One News
will be replaced with smoking videos
of outgoing cabinet ministers
at length (and with great enthusiasm)
feasting on the more excitable parts
of Apple CEO Tim Cook.
For in the new jurisdiction
the powers that were will be made admit
their true religion, and then set free.

There will be no lowlights on the nine o'clock
news claiming there was hardly anyone there.
The theme song will not be written by Phil Coulter
or Dustin, nor be sung by Linda Martin, Westlife,
or Foster and Allen. And it will not be available later
on the RTE iPlayer.

It will not be right back
after a message from an actor in Killinaskully
you can't quite name promising to kill
99% of known bacteria, including those
that'll make Michael O'Leary's ass eventually decompose.
The new rising will hand the Lewis sub-machine gun
to you, your increasingly discontented cat,
and your most eccentric auntie.

This rising will not be available later on the RTE iPlayer.
This rising will be live,
gobshite, live.

Sympathy for The Sympathetic

after Jagger and Richards

When you phone to say you're caught
in the Kyber pass or Kalahari desert,
I won't ask how you got there.

I'll be in the ambulance holding
your hot pink hand the day
the parachute jump fails
to cure your fear of heights.

I'll say "poor you" with my whole face
and mean it, when the affair
with your mother-in-law
ends unpleasantly, or
they won't let you smoke
cigars in the oncology day ward.

Too busy remembering the whiskeys
I bought George Best
to pass judgement on anything.

Next time you find yourself
with a biker gang in a wooded area
fifty miles north of Moscow and
things take an unexpected turn
for the worse, you've got
my number.

I Am Pleased To Congratulate On Behalf Of The People Of Ireland

after Enda Kenny

Donald J. Duck on his election
as forty fifth, and possibly final,
President of that great entity
traditionally known as the United
States which, admittedly,
by the time he's finished with it,
will likely be called something else.

In the heat of battle President-elect
Duck has said things
which have left him with bridges to build
with certain people, such as Mexican
transsexuals, and women
who don't want him,
or anyone politically
associated with him even thinking
about grabbing their
vaginas, or the vaginas of their
friends, mothers-in-law, or
as yet unborn children.

We think today in particular of
Secretary of State Clinton,
though only very briefly,
for eaten parsnips are quickly
digested, and we must move on.
Democracy (and, for that matter,
dictatorship) have their own outcomes.
This being the case, if President-elect
Duck wants to build a crazy golf course
in every front garden on this island,

I will work closely with compliant
urban district councils, sympathetic
journalists, and members of the judiciary
to have the necessary planning
fast-tracked.

And rest assured, every opportunity
that presents itself, either
I or one of my Ministers will be there
to shake his hand,
or any other part of his anatomy
President-elect, Donald J.
Duck, wants shaken.

What They Don't Know Is

after Dennis O'Driscoll

That this cannot be avoided by everyone wearing protective glasses.
That the contents of their half-full cups are about to evaporate.
That the University will remain closed until further notice.
That Kim Kardashian's arse has been abolished.
That the idea of tomorrow is suddenly quaint as a dinner plate
    made in West Germany.
That the price of house insurance just went up ten thousand per cent.
That the lack of reception on their mobile phones isn't because
    they're going through a tunnel.
That even the hairstyle of the Fox News anchor woman is no
    longer perfect.
That Adolf is now the second most hated politician in history.
That the station at which this train terminates no longer exists.
That the priest who'll give them last rites is just a guy in an outfit
    his brother recently wore to a fancy dress.
That God is a skeleton who knows everything and will one day talk.

from Tax

after Michael Noonan

In the income tax arena
I am introducing a scheme:

whereby a fifty year old man
living in, for example,
Galway, will still be able to claim
for his increasingly rickety right knee
here in Ireland, but allowed register,
for tax purposes,
his far more profitable left leg in Jersey.

He'll be able to claim relief here on his wonky eye
but will only have to pay tax on the good one
at whatever the rate is in Luxembourg.

His three sets of dentures, all twenty six
fillings and those two root canals
will continue to be deductible here,
though he'll now pay tax
on what's left of his actual
teeth in Bermuda.

The good fifty percent of his lungs
he'll be allowed set up
as an independent company
in the British Virgin Islands,
while the useless half will legally
continue to be Irish.

His nausea will remain ours,
though his enormous appetite
will now officially live on the more
glutton-friendly Isle of Man.

His beleaguered liver will continue
to be officially resident here,
while his still superefficient
bowels will spend enough time in Switzerland
to pay (hardly any) tax there.

The scar above his left buttock,
acquired when he toppled through a glass door
backwards, circa nineteen seventy three,
will continue to be deductible here,
while the balance of his bum –
in surprisingly good condition for a man his age,
though he says so himself – declares
its vast income at an office
in Wilmington, Delaware.

Elsewhere, I am extending the relief on brown leather
trousers and industrial strength lawnmowers
for fat couples with Anglo-Norman sounding names
in the better bits of Kildare for another five years.
There is agreement across the political consensus
it's essential such people are given sufficient incentives
to keep doing
whatever it is they supposedly do.

Conference Speech

"What's my vision for Britain? My philosophy? My approach?
Today I want to answer that question very directly."
     Theresa May

Who am I? And what on earth am I doing here?
Let me be clear. Each time I stand up to speak
as your Prime Minister, the church organist at Midsomer
kills again: the village florist gets it savagely
across the back of the head with a cast iron frying pan
that's been in the family since seventeen seventy six;
or her lover, the sexton, turns up strip-jack-naked
at the bottom of the better variety of slurry pit…

In my Britain the brothels that serve
next year's Conservative Party conference
will only employ girls with 'Best of British' tattooed
tastefully across their lower backs. Trust me,
when all the relevant members of my cabinet
have had their faces sat on for a fee
by Staffordshire's finest, the British people will see
we, as a government, are ready to grasp
this once in a generation chance for change.

I will glue our United Kingdom back together,
and never let divisive nationalists,
with the exception of those here amongst us today,
tear us asunder. To this end,
the children of Dundee and Kirkcaldy
will be made recite every morning before Latin
the collected works of Rudyard Kipling;
and every homeowner south of Rickmansworth
on a salary over thrice the national average
will be given a toy Glaswegian each
with a tiny can of Irn Bru preinstalled, courtesy
of the new Department of Citizenship & Ethnic Integrity.

We are not just a party for the big people,
the sort who know what's in the compromising photographs
the average person must never be allowed see;
we also rely on the votes of those many millions
of little people who believe in
what the big people have in store for them.

Come with me as we rise
to meet this challenge and take
each of them – be they gay
or straight, white or a bit yellow,
complete slap head or hairy all over –
coldly by the gullet
and give them the shaking
we know they deserve.

Governing Council Statement on Recent Non-standard Measures

after Zbigniew Herbert & the ECB statement of 11/12/2015

Since June the Governing Council have adopted a series of new malignancy enhancing measures, our aim to counter growing risks of a too prolonged period of successful DNA repair across the Euro area as a whole. Those measures have included reducing key anti-cancer treatments to levels below zero, introducing an incentive package – specifically our Targeted Long-Term Sarcoma Re-invigoration Programme (TLSP) – and expanding our Tumour Intensification Initiative (TII). These non-standard measures were decided against the backdrop of invasiveness and metastasis at the weaker end of what can typically be observed at the onset of such crises, and, from summer of 2014 onwards, heightened downside risks to the carcinogenesis outlook and a concrete threat of cell stability.

This complex package of measures has led to a significant increase in nuclear matrix protein 22 and carcinoembryonic antigens in recent blood and urine samples and should thereby continue to contribute to the rapidity of cell division and the appearance of new growths in non-peripheral areas. Early evidence confirms current policies are delivering measurable results, in particular improving conditions faced by non-small cell neoplasms– of all sizes – and individual cells thinking of entering the indefinitely recurring mitosis stage.

Starting with concerns regarding non-proliferation of Aflatoxin B1, Benzene, and the human papilloma virus, we have overcome market concerns about shortages by injecting liquidity into this market, and making said liquidity available cheaply in jars of what look like peanut butter. Occurrences have increased, even in Member States previously largely unaffected, in the wake of our policy measures. Before the launch of the June 2014 Free Vinyl Bromide for the Peripheral (FVBFTP) package the bulk of the deterioration had not been transmitted to the millions of potentially rapidly reproducing cells existent in households across all vulnerable Member States. From May last year (when markets started to anticipate our pro-cyclical Free Radical package) until October this year, however, high end pharmaceutical stocks have moved higher, up more than 10 per cent across the Euro area in aggregate. This process has been assisted by a number of mergers and acquisitions in the sector, and evidence that the introduction of large amounts of Vinyl Bromide into the bloodstreams of the very elderly and the small under laboratory conditions is impacting the situation more rapidly than we had anticipated.

To put that in perspective, Governing Council staff estimates suggest that an increase of the standard dioxin and cigarette smoke infusion rates by around 100 fold in June 2014 would have been required to achieve a similar effect on the amount of cold meat delivered to the walk-in refrigerator hook. Moreover, neuroblastoma rates among ten year olds rose by some 110-140 per cent in major vulnerable Member States, suggesting that the pass-through of the Governing Council's policy stance has become stronger in those countries that were costing us most and where inappropriate cell division was slowest.

The improvement in hospitals' supplies of plant alkaloids and mustard gas derivatives has been further empowered by a welcome month-on-month decline in survival rates among the generally unnecessary, spurred by our measures.

The Governing Council has reinforced this by putting strong upward pressure on overnight hospital bed yields and thereby increasing the attractiveness of flat-pack coffins, in which the health sector is now making long overdue investment. Up forty percent in the last quarter, with a steeper than average growth curve in states situated on the Mediterranean. Likely shortages of chipboard and other impure timber products for easy construction of same is now considered the most important medium term impediment to finalising both a full recovery and the necessary state-led mopping up operation until we can get things back how they were immediately before diagnosis day.

The So-Called World

Outside, the so-called sun hangs defining itself in the self-styled sky.
In here, the self-styled cat on the so-called window sill quietly
completes its inventory of so-called crows
that taunt it from tree tops they pretend to own.
Online, the self-styled New York Times says
the so-called President of the self-styled United States
has vowed to drive so-called Islamic State – who last night introduced
twenty seven self-styled rock fans to the so-called
Kalashnikov or forty two
so-called tourists to the self-styled suicide-belt,
you can't quite remember which – from their remaining strongholds
and into the open where within a couple
of what the so-called President is calling months
the so-called Central Intelligence Agency can cleanse
its few remaining adherents
from the so-called surface
of this so-called Earth.

Pictures of Unfamiliars

after Carolyn Forché

Beamed into one's living room via satellite,
or framed in syndicated photographs
on the quality papers' foreign pages, even
their black or missing front teeth
have a strange beauty.

The shanty town dwellers of La Paz,
in their hand woven red and green ponchos,
carry themselves in a fashion
which puts to shame the post office queue
scraggy mother of two, with change
in her slovenly wallet for lottery tickets,
but not shampoo.

Nothing against the locals.
But the skeletal colosseum cats have a grace
which the one I ran over on my way
to this morning's Amnesty
International meeting absolutely lacked,
even before my brand new
Good Year Assurance tires ironed flat
its entirely unremarkable pelvis.

The ongoing pain of the Yazidi women
and the entire Choctaw nation (every generation)
is best struggled with over a fair trade salad
in one of the more radical tea shops
on Sandymount Strand.

In comparison, one admits,
our local Others - with their dole
day drunkenness, and lack of imagination
which has seen them prosaically wander the roads
these past thousand years – just
don't cut the whole grain mustard.

When they start mouthing *Civil Rights*
and municipal water cannon, or
police batons get over enthusiastic
on their irresponsibly positioned skulls,
people like me will feel forced to pass by
on the other side, checking our messages
for pictures of unfamiliars being
deliciously maltreated
anywhere else.

On The New Parliamentary Rump
In The Absence of Mandatory Reselection

after John Milton

Because you have shrugged off all sentiment,
like a convention of businessmen, each in turn,
successfully losing his boxer shorts
at an after party that will, in due course,
be put in the accounts under 'miscellaneous';
he who is of sufficient wallet, and ugliness,
to purchase for himself exclusive access
to a slightly soiled Jerry Hall now raises
you up in his pages, and on TV screens
that answer to him, as the sort of
Lancashire lass or professional
Welsh accent who's happy
to continue to rule on behalf
of those who must rule, even
if the other guy wins the vote,
with his sandals, his allotment,
his mindless allegiance
to those who haven't had
the beef cheek this century,
going on ever, and won't be
having it anytime soon, if you
and those on whose behalf
you hope to administer
get your way, as you will,
if insufficient use is made
of liberating axe and guillotine.

The Sudden Thaw & What
It's Doing To You

At the finish of the recent ice age, when
history suddenly wasn't over anymore
and another future began to be written

you were the first daffodil to push its face
up through earth frozen twenty five years
before those with stronger stems followed
to better face what the wind would bring.

Today, you're outraged the resurrected
Allende didn't consult you on his media strategy
while the coup plotters were bombing
the presidential palace from the air, though all
the while you left your smart phone on
to take his call.

When the new round of mechanised killing
really gets going – somewhere near Calais,
or due south of Budapest – you'll make it
a latest video for The Guardian,
speak earnestly to camera
about the appalling roughness of some
of the lavatory paper there,
and post it on Twitter.

Can't be easy
when no one but you gets it:
we'll only defeat great evil
by taking it out for coffee
and seeing its point of view.
Over the years you become its new
more persuasive face.

On The Departure From Office Of Barack Obama

You are the bed we'd happily have slept in,
if only we'd managed to assemble you
but there was always a bit missing.
So you forced us to spend the night
admiring the pictures in the brochure.

The exquisite wrapping
on a box with zilch in it
except a mildly amusing joke
you had written for you
but delivered with such charisma
it set people whispering
that you're the political wing
of Earth, Wind, and Fire
without the heavy ideology.

The skinny kid
with the funny name who dared
hope in the face of adversity
and on your watch
Wall Street got the biggest
hard-on in its history
and you kept feeding it
interest free Viagra.

For the rest of us
you're the medicine
that tasted excellent
until we woke up almost dead.

January 20th 2017

Surprised By Joy (whatever her name is)

after William Wordsworth

Just found out today, I've a sister not
named Purity who doesn't live in Gravesend, Kent
    or hate cats, or scream when she finds
a tarantula in the corner of the shower
    but cups it in her pinkies
finds for it a cottage in the Cotswolds,
    visits it there in the holidays;

who doesn't light farthing candles
    to the three-in-one god
of Proper Order, Common Sense
    and ruining other people's Christmases;
or have a signed photograph of Rod
    Stewart she looks at not
nearly often enough;

    who wasn't shocked
when they took Ken Barlow away
    or found human remains
under the school principal's
    clean shaven lawn;

who'd gamble not one Drachma
    on the afterlife but believes fanatically
in a place called
    Wait While I Get My Cardigan.
A no longer but once
    young lady about whom,
right now, for legal reasons,
    I can say no more than this.

Things To Do In Galway Before You Again Decide Not To Shoot Yourself

Take up smoking other people's cigarettes and wear
a beret you found on the Ballybane bus.
Write a Last Will and Testament in which you bequeath
your lungs to your least favourite busker.
Get given a banjo on someone else's
fifty first birthday and fully intend
to learn how to play it.

Launch an online petition angrily calling
for more of the same.
Organise a fundraising concert in aid
of yourself, headlined by a guy who once met Peter, Paul
& Mary. Carry a concealed photo of a young Lord Haw Haw
in the breast pocket of the shabby three piece
you wear at weekends and consider

a career in broadcasting. If male, nickname
that thing in your underpants
the late Bishop Browne; if female,
erect a sign officially
re-naming your equal and opposite bits
John F. Kennedy Square.

Become an elderly crank in pyjama pants
who once owned a craft shop.
Try our range of face creams
Druid's Semen Number One, Two & Three.
Wake up shouting about homeopathy,
El Salvador, Palestine.

Skulk up back streets face down-
beat as a bad turn out
at a charity event for athlete's
foot. Visit the Abbey and buy a Mass card.
Send it to yourself by registered post,
so tomorrow at least
the world will have some sympathy.

Not Red Nor A Rose, No

after Robert Burns

Our love was a dandelion cut mercifully
short by a lawnmower. Our words,
a concert at which it was best to turn up
late and leave early. Arrogant as the heir
to one of the biggest fortunes in Miami accused
of murdering a prostitute;
our plans were shallow as talk
of the next Men Without Hats reunion.
From the off we were an international
political crisis in the making. We were history
coming up out of the drains.

Our promises to each other
were a spare set of dentures
trampled underfoot by burglars.
The story of our break up:
a long, filthy handkerchief
it's taken me twenty years
to unwind from my pocket
and place for safekeeping
under my pillow.

Epithalamium

Now she will feel mostly rain,
like a long wet whip put
across her face by an angry drunk,
for each of you will be exposure for the other.

Now there will be this aloneness,
for each of you will be absence to the other.
You are two persons with little life before you.
Go now to your big house behind its gate
to enter into the days
of your homelessness together,
where he will squeak about
on the PVC couch
he recently gave himself as a present,
in his brand new leather pants,

and mature to become
what the long brown coats
exiting the mortuary
years from now will call:
the terrible circumstances
in which she did her best.

To Whom It Definitely Concerns

after Adrian Mitchell

I was knocked down by a Lie today.
I asked the Lie who told it, and it put its finger
on a picture of you.
     So sink your ankles in concrete.
     And get back your stutter.

Heard the doorbell screaming like a toothache.
Couldn't face answering it.
     So fill your ears with candlewax.
     Sink your ankles in concrete.
     And get back your stutter.

Every time I close my eyes all I see are flames.
Nothing to do but lie here, saying your name.
     So cover your eyes with onion.
     Fill your ears with candlewax.
     Sink your ankles in concrete.
     And get back your stutter.

I smell something burning, hope it's just your house.
And you spend 'til forever going through the ruins.
     So stuff your nostrils with Tampons.
     Cover your eyes with onion.
     Fill your ears with candlewax.
     Sink your ankles in concrete.
     And get back your stutter.

Where were you at the time of the Lie?
Down the Dog and Duck talking workers' rights.
     So wire your testicles up to the mains.
     Stuff your nostrils with Tampons.
     Cover your eyes with onion.
     Fill your ears with candlewax.
     Sink your ankles in concrete.
     And get back your stutter.

You grab the reputation and you roll it around in sewage.
You take the human being, and you laugh about it in the pub.
    So scrub your skin with children.
    Wire your testicles up to the mains.
    Stuff your nostrils with Tampons.
    Cover your eyes with onion.
    Fill your ears with candlewax.
    Sink your ankles in concrete.
    And stutter me this.

The Undoing

First, I take off my hair
and put it back in the clear
plastic bag it came in, then peel
off my eyebrows and leave
them on the bedside locker,
like two recently deceased
black caterpillars. One
by one, I clip off finger
and toenails, deposit them
safely in the matchbox they
traditionally spend the night in.
I tear off tongue, then bollocks
and stuff them into the pint glass
I use to give visitors
a nice drink of water;
unzip my skin skull to foot
and leave it sag on a clothes hanger
from the closet door. I spoon
out my eyes and bathe them in the usual
small cup of malt vinegar. Then making sure
to leave the door unlocked,
lay my laughing skeleton
back on the bed in the hope
someone undoes themselves
by accidentally on purpose
catching me like this.

Inappropriate Comparisons

If I could be bothered, I'd compare you
to a television presenter rubbing Nutella
into Chris De Burgh's buttocks; say
that you are only slightly less likeable
than a twice defeated election candidate who enjoys
hanging around funeral parlours;
that your words are accurate and beautiful
as boiled eggs peeled and tossed out windows
at random passing cars; that your smile
is all the sugar you didn't take in your tea
during Lent; that you're almost as lovely
as the economist, who was wrong about everything,
giving his bald patch its daily sprinkle
of bulls' urine. But I'd rather not
acknowledge the ongoing tragedy
of your continued existence.

from

The Boy With No Face

(2005)

To Hell And Back Again

Now that, at last,
you seem to have found yourself
you often long to be lost again,
to drift down a throbbing street
in the thick of the afternoon
at the centre of your own solar system,
to shillyshally for hours
over a mug of tea and a slice of toast
in some greasy-spoon,
where no-one would even dream
of asking for a cappuccino or a latté,
or, better still, not to bother
leaving your filthy flat all day at all
but, when the last ray of sun has, finally, gone away,
to shamble down to the kebab house
for a pickled onion and a portion of chips
because you don't have the cash
to use the brothel around the back.
But if you slip from these shackles,
your future which opens up
like a new continent that, of course,
must be conquered,
this clean living which sometimes
fits you like a collar and tie on a boiling hot day
at one of those awkward family occasions,
if you go back to all that liberty, to all that Hell,
you might not make it back again this time.

By Five o'clock

Your last day at the office gone down the drain,
you're null and void once again.
On Quay Street nothing but loud-mouthed money.
You live in a city—no a country—
run by idiots you went to school with.
Your father'd put his finger
precisely where you've gone wrong,
if he wasn't off in a mobile home
with her from number five.
But, in a week or so,
the up-side of idleness will strike you.
A universe of time for nothing but writing!
Your satires will suffer as you run out of characters
on a thin diet of teletext news.
Your girlfriend will dump you.
(Your lover won't phone.)
The blonde in the bookshop won't laugh at your jokes.
You'll visit your mother more and more often,
become what the girls at the office
call "the Norman Bates sort". Look in the mirror!
The smirk has slipped, Sunny Jim.
The face on the floor is definitely yours.

To certain lyric poets

This lyric poet sees
his own reflection everywhere.
Even, 'her hair on the pillow
like freshly fallen snow',
is there to let us know
he still gets laid,
although, in this case,
she probably passed
through Robert Graves's hands first.
But we should be gentle
when we mention
"the narrowness of his range",
that lovely little phrase the critics invented,
a device to side-step saying, instead,
"he only ever talks about himself".
Every poem is another love-letter
to the person to whom
his whole life's work
has been dedicated.
He's been known
to agonise for hours
over a single word
and each one of them
is precisely meant
because, to him,
words are beautiful things,
flowers to be arranged
around an altar to his ego.

I am Ireland

after Pádraic Pearse

I am Ireland:
I am the love-child of Brian Keenan and John Waters.
I drive Lebanese terrorists and Sinéad O'Connor bonkers.
I will go on forever.

Great my glory:
I am Enya's next album
and Michael Flatley's other testicle rolled into one.

Great my shame:
I am Frank McCourt's next book
and, even worse, I'm his brother.

I am Ireland:
I am Louis Walsh waiting for the Milli Vanilli to hit the fan.
I keep a hyena in my front garden and I am ready!

President Robinson Pays Homage to Lord Haw Haw, 21 October 1996

after Paul Durcan and Francis Stuart

On the stroke of midnight,
during a secret ceremony in Arás an Uachtaráin,
President Robinson placed the Collar of Gold
around the neck of Lord Haw Haw
(the broadcaster formerly known as William Joyce)
"It's a comfortable fit",
Galway's most famous bag of bones was heard to remark.
Paying her homage to Haw Haw,
speaking stridently and without a script,
just like Haw Haw himself used to do in the old days,
Mrs Robinson stated that when her own thinking
had been making its shapes, Haw Haw's example
had proved invaluable.
It taught her the crucial role of the individual in history.
"His is an awkward, an uncomfortable voice."
In response, Haw Haw, after bowing to the President,
stated that, as a citizen of The City of The Tribes,
he felt honoured and proud.
A relaxed President relaxing at his side, posed for photographs
with the skeleton of the legendary broadcaster.

A Postcard from Minneapolis

"Lots of ghosts, cars and junk
but strangely little history
here in old America…" And then swiftly on
to all your favourite whinges.
"Don't wanna be here. Don't even drink beer…"

But as your card to me shot
postmarked from the machine
—September 10th 21.53—an alarm-clock
somewhere was being well and truly set.
Luggage. Tickets. Everything ready. A man
muttering something in Arabic. And soon
floating in from a neighbouring room:
'This is the ten o'clock news.'

Then from Greenwich Village to San Diego
the streets slowly emptying, until
—everything standing momentarily still—
America's a movie set, with actors
everywhere waiting for the man
to shout: 'Lights. Camera. Action!'

Café Du Journal

"I feel like a European."
"I know what you mean",
the Czech waitress tells him,
and then just stands there,
dazzled by the headlights
of his Andy Williams smile,
as he eyes up every square inch
of her autonomous republic:
from the Bohemia of her behind
to the Prague Spring of her cleavage:
in that oh so casual 'I only want
the Sudetenland' manner of his.

A Real Galwegian

Because when you watch the woman
sitting next to you writing an e-mail
in what looks like Korean, or find yourself asking
someone called Candy from Saskatchewan
for two bagels with cream-cheese,

it occasionally still hits you; how it's
like the blink of an eyelid since, down this street,
the coffee was rotten, and a night out
just a pint of sad *Smithwicks* eventually
emerging in a withered hand
from a back-street hatch, a barman telling

a complaining Yank how the lock broken
on that toilet door has been that way
for nearly twenty years, and not
a single shit stolen yet.

Desperate Weather

If it wasn't Linz, 1906,
but here and now, there he'd sit,
huddled at a table in *Le Graal*,
a same time, same place, most nights,
usual table type of guy,
to whom you'd maybe nod
or mutter something, here so often,
you can't but know him,
an edge of the picture
all night wind-bag sort of character,
his audience of one typically far
more taken with the waitress's arse.
Nothing to his name, which somehow slips you,
but a lottery ticket and a date with FÁS.
The best parts of most days, he snores them away,
late afternoon catches him
with paints and canvas, *a budding genius*,
a derivative style all of his own.
And, Lord preserve us, he writes "poetry",
is influenced by Wagner but mostly Mother.
His usual table sometimes taken. "It's okay if I sit here?
The name's Hitler." "You look familiar."
"Isn't it desperate weather." "Yes, desperate weather."

A Brief History of Those Who Made Their Point Politely And Then Went Home

On this day of tear-gas in Seoul
and windows broken at *Dickins & Jones*,
I can't help wondering why a history
of those, who made their point politely
and then went home, has never been written.

Those who, in the heat of the moment,
never dislodged a policeman's helmet,
never blocked the traffic or held the country to ransom.
Someone should ask them: "Was it all worth it?"

All those proud men and women, who never
had the National Guard sent in against them;
who left everything exactly as they found it,
without adding as much as a scratch to the paintwork;
who no-one bothered asking: "Are you or have you ever been?",
because we all knew damn well they never ever were.

Else

However hard I try
I just can't shake this defeated feeling,
fallen into such an utter disarray,
I'm a cheek with no smack on it,
a white sheet with no KKK in it,
a page of pornography
and not a single confirmed sighting of an arse in the bare,
or anything better for that or any other matter.
I must have gone to a wrong place with a wrong clock,
like a guillotine with no neck in it,
a leopard-skin with no slapper in it,
I'm a wrong thing wandered into an erroneous context,
a punch with no face waiting to meet it at the other end,
all I can do only is to continue now
and be one own half of something completely else.

January

for Susan

The ashtrays need emptying
and the cat's been sick.
The mice in the attic are giving out stink.
As we watch our breath drift
across the kitchen, central heating
is a luxury as distant as trays
of oysters at the Galway Races.
The year struggles to its feet,
like a lamb stranded in deep snow.
Strange then to think, this evening in Siberia,
that these are the good old days;
I, the unknown "poet and critic",
you, the next F. Scott Fitzgerald,
up all night, putting the world to wrong;
writing new versions of old songs.

Almost Invisible

When winter's chill and pallid spectre
ripples across the horizon
to thrust itself once more
upon a gilded autumn's final fling,
and to roughly wrap dead hands around
the sultry traces of those lingering summer days,

> the rust-red leaves in swollen gardens,
> the buoyant banter of candent girls,
> who pulsed the wild streets
> aggravating the symptoms,

then he will, again, venture from his shady hollow
to hang on the frigid corners of unfrequented lanes
thickly stained in the jet-black of dusk. Almost invisible.

Letter to a Friend about Girls

after Philip Larkin

What losers we were when it came to girls.
'Pull up to my bumper baby, drive it in between'
played soundtrack to the wet dreams
of small, inconsequential fellas, the likes of us.
And we're talking small on an almost monumental scale.
In duffel coats and awful glasses
we shuffled around the edges of other people's parties
all through the eighties,
gawking down in the general direction
of our stupid, stupid shoes.
If charisma could be distilled,
ours would have been measured
in somewhat less than millilitres.
So small, we barely existed.

On the rare occasions when opportunity
—the tastiest variety—put herself there
to be availed of and there was nothing for it
but to press the advantage all the way home,
we either failed to spot the most obvious signals
—our radar were useless at picking incoming aircraft up—
or else managed to inexplicably miss.
She grinned through the worst jokes
and was clearly prepared to overlook that duffel coat,
but the score on the board stubbornly somehow stayed zero.
The goal could be yawning wide open
and still the ball would either trickle
pathetically wide or go sailing miles over.
And just what exactly were we supposed to say
as another cut-price night at *The Oasis* declined
(with no bachelor flat to which she might be lured back)?
"Let's explore the universe with my last fifty pence piece.
If I empty my pockets perhaps I could stretch as far as a kebab."

Blackhole

This is the place where an old man with a twisted neck
falters on his way down a long pathway
to his privatised death in some musty, dark corner of a room.

This is the place where young men come out
into the shadows behind cemetery walls
to paint swastikas on headstones
and play football with skulls.

This is the place where council estates come complete
with built in big dogs and gunshots,
where a dull sun bakes the furnace air
as tower-block windows give that careless look
that only tranquillised eyes can throw,
where concrete thrusts pick the nose of the sky
as rubbish blows on the slow route to the paper heart of it all,
where the empty hours of the afternoon just get longer
    and longer,
where a drunk spunks out poison about Pakis and
    seven-year-olds
run junkie messages in Camelot House for carpet-knifed men
who carve reminders on the door,
where a wheel-chaired man belts the floor with his
    paranoid stick
and someone screams at a bare-knuckled wall
after the key-meter ran out,
where schizophrenics sit in timeless cafés
as matted hair women join pointless queues,
where a crack in the door shooter points up a bailiff nostril
as pools of liquid are in corners of the lift,
where police murders fall down stairs of convenience
and onto page nineteen,
where concealed Stanley-knives lurk
around scuttling cash-point machines
as lethal impressions hang
around the bus-shelter in the distance,

where asylum eyes poke out into the frantic spectre of the dusk
as endless discussions chase their tales
out through bizarre suicidal windows,
down to earth, where the dawn shines an angry light
into the bald face of the morning as nameless
blood stains another pavement,
where you could write slogans in the grime on the billboards
but no-one knows what to say now,
where arteries are clogged in North Circular bottlenecks
as ghettoblasters beat obscenities into the heads of grey
    old women,
where no-one asks the question
why do you write depressing poetry?

Here there are no nature walks,
no buttercups nor wild roses flourish.
No ripe autumn roads of blackberry brambles
bouncing along with a spring in their step.
Only poisoned grass by the railway.
Only grey-black slush dissolving the memory
of the last pure flake of snow.

This is the place where the city looks out through
    exhausted eyes,
where sweaty streets are all dressed up
in tasteless rectangular grey,
where day dreams flicker in café tea mugs
as cheapskate hotels rent out rooms by the hour.

This is the place,
just another sore in the mouth of the metropolis
where hope has been given an execution cigarette,
where it's very much a case of c'est la vie
as you straggle into the abyss of the echoing streets
at an insane hour after talking it all through.
This is the place from where no light escapes.

from

Time Gentlemen, Please

(2008)

Foreboding

Once more
the endless Monday to Sunday
and back around again, the days
content mostly just to be
a small dog peeing against the same old tree.
So why then do you get the feeling
that the future's about to leap at you,
like a baboon with a hatchet
from a man-hole or a closet, screaming
something which can only mean
'This is the end of the old regime'?

From the future, a postcard home

After the imagined ice-cream clouds
and warm blue rain, the frost bristling
picturesque grass, the parties
where the women were topless, the men
all wearing tuxedos; each day's

metallic tap-water taste. Outside
the chapped lips and tea-cosy hats
of a Winter afternoon's typical trajectory.
In your head, these dissonant fingers
still plinking along with some mad monologue
banging its gong. Outside

the freezing fog bothering their nostrils.
In your head, the essential details
of an August evening: the angle
of her bra-strap as the books
came tumbling, the minus signs

massing at the border. Elsewhere
nothing now but the present
as the cat gives up sniffing your sad
cheeseless hands, and goes back
to catching the giant mice
of its dreams.

The Couple Upstairs

Your husband's last set of golf-clubs
in their vest of cobwebs; and the chair
you've sat in since Jimmy Carter
often empty now, as you tumble away to a life
of medicine, mash and Sunday night
nephews. Moments though

when every sound upstairs
is sex: every rustle across a table-top
some ecstasy of underwear
whistling to the floor, every whisper
of a floorboard her once again, turning
her pale backside to the sky; times

when all he has to do is drop
his *Penguin Book of Poetry From
Britain and Ireland Since 1945*
and you shudder at the thought of them
about to commit an unnatural act
on a Tuesday afternoon. And your stick's

suddenly frantic against the ceiling,
or you're ringing the bell
to tell them to stop, 'til you settle
back to a big, black afterwards now
fractured only by this last lightning
across its sky.

Tuesday

Her still away and the town
all East winds and tonsillitis, as you come
back for a quiet night in not playing
with yourself, but instead get the loud
catastrophe of a friend, whose wife's
finally told him: "Time for Teletubbie fuck off",
meowing on your garage roof. Hours
then of him determined to see nothing
in the coffee cup but the absence now
of anyone to help him to the exit
in the event of darkness. Later,

his blood black with caffeine and whiskey,
he swears on *The Koran*, *Bible*
and *Little Book of Complete Bollocks* to be more
from now on than an instrument
in any woman's orchestra. And suddenly all you can see
is the promise for him of a long future
of cough syrup and scoreless draws, as he goes on
to share various caravans with guys
with mad, grey, heavy metal hair and perhaps
once a year have an out of underpants experience
with a woman twice his age. By midnight

you're about to tell him
you'd rather wake up with
the late Leonid Brezhnev, than have to listen
to any more of this, but at the last moment
keep your sympathetic head, because
as the proverb says: "Mock not, for tomorrow
you too may have your bare arse
turned to the sun."

My Militant Tendency

It's nineteen eighty two and I know everything.
Hippies are people who always end up asking
Charles Manson to sing them another song.
I'd rather be off putting some fascist through
a glass door arseways, but being fifteen,
have to mow the lawn first. Last year,

Liverpool meant football; now
it's the Petrograd of the British Revolution.
Instead of masturbation, I find socialism.
While others dream of businessmen bleeding
in basements; I promise to abolish double-chemistry class
the minute I become Commissar. In all of this
there is usually a leather jacket involved. I tell

cousin Walter and his lovely new wife, Elizabeth,
to put their aspirations in their underpants
and smoke them; watch

my dad's life become a play:
Sit Down In Anger.

Conversation with a Former Self

Not for you New York or Paris,
a career, perhaps, depicting fashionable
women in their boudoirs. Instead
the bare chapel of your garage flat;

the sour milk and lavender; watching
the cups crack like marriages. You always
a deserving cause rattling its box. The vast,
unforgiving tundra of your politics

stretching on 'til posterity
has your legacy
                    crumpled in its fist:
the bible-studies righteousness
and way you let the world
mop the floor with your head,

until it was a simple case of go quietly
on that pink ladies mountain bike,
or be taken away in this brown
paper-bag.

Dad

On yellow evenings
in a country which no longer exists,
we ignore each other
over deceased cups of coffee.
Until I shatter
the pristine silence:
announce my opposition
to the trickledown theory, or
the concept of right and wrong
as you understand it; or say
all things considered
this would be a good time for
the world to end.

Sometimes you bark back:
that in my world without rules
Ian Brady would probably tour Europe
promoting his autobiography
Everybody Gets What They Deserve:
"The author will be available afterwards
to take children from the audience";
and never mind the big opinions,
with my Leaving Cert the only job
I'm fit for, in a country
which no longer exists, is meeting men
in hotels for small change.

But mostly you abscond to give
some innocent shrub
a skinhead haircut; allow me
to keep contradicting myself
until I find out what it is
I'm trying to say.

Ending Up

Outside the Burger King on *Piccadilly* Circus
that's where I met him first, always itching
to quote *Socialism or Catastrophe*
but *Homage to Catalonia* was his favourite book.
In different times he'd have died in Spain.
In the autumn of '88 he married her instead;
ended up on the Essex side of the M25.

In his prime he'd talk all night
—how it would all have been so different—
"if only Rosa Luxembourg took my advice."
I got his dog-eared copy
of *The Ragged Trousered Philanthropists*
the day he went into human resource management;
his *Communist Manifesto* the day he boarded the plane
for a piece of the action on the new Moscow stock exchange.

Their marriage was one of those rare soap operas
which no-one bothers to watch—
the acting wooden, the dialogue nonsensical—
in the end they stayed together;
kept those perfect carpets
out of the divorce courts.
Everything was in order
that Tuesday evening last October.
He took his shoes off, as usual,
at the front door.

Somewhere between the end
of *The Channel Four News*
and the signature tune for *Friends*—
in a matter of seconds—
he went without a struggle;
was dead in the chair
when she got out of the shower;
had one of those English funerals
with no-one at them. A curtain opened
and he was smoke.

Catastrophe comes in many guises
and not always with the strident voice
of a doomed member of the Baader-Meinhoff.
It also arrives, more quietly,
on the Essex side of the M25.

The Great Depression

Since love took its clown questions
and vomit-coloured clothes down
the fire escape that dusk, the woman,
who once put the *quoi*
into Je ne sais quoi, has gone
from the city of caffeine
and glittering websites
                              to wander late
the boulevards of Stalintown handing
out yellow-pack tuna fish to the poor, her face
like a ruined bank-holiday weekend, her talk
like LSD and downers in a country
where it's always Tuesday.

The Candidate

Who, without opening his mouth, tells you
that, for him, it was stay there forever
making up worlds that will never be
in a side-street with nothing to offer
but the monthly *Tea-dance and sing-along*
for the over fifty-fives, or grow up to be
Junior Minister for Counter-Terrorism;

that you can scowl all you want,
his suit will just keep beaming back, now
the miracle of modern dentistry has given the boy
with the shrieking red t-shirt
and mouthful of bombed-out teeth
this ice white New Labour smile;

that as you stand there,
looking suddenly old in the Post Office queue
used, by now, to the idea of not being played
by Jack Nicholson in the film of your life
that'll never be made;

he daydreams he's signing the order
that'll send you away across the courtyard
to have your head shaved
by the Anti-Everything Police.

Reasons for doing The John Walker Lindh

"John Walker Lindh, a 20-year-old Californian, was captured while fighting for the Taliban."
    CNN

Because there must be more
to life than basketball;
Habitat for Inhumanity; and
marrying women named Sue
as in *for damages*. Because
your parents increasingly sound
like strange beings from
a far, plastic universe.

Because you'd rather go
where the coffins are leaky
and the summers hot, fight
the bad fight at Mazaar-E-Shariff,
than suffer another Level 5 Christmas
at the *Radisson*, or be remembered
as someone who overcame huge
advantages to achieve
total obscurity.

Firewood

A bone field fifty metres by fifty.
It's problematic to describe this as genocide.
I gather firewood at eight o'clock in the morning.
My son clings to my dress. Men in uniforms
with military insignia stop their car
and throw him into a fire. Then five of them
one after the other. I am paralysed.
It's problematic to describe this as genocide.
The solution is not military intervention. We demand
the US keep its hands off Sudan.
Children start jumping out windows
when the Janjaweed come into the school.
The police begin firing. Everyone,
mainly babies and the elderly,
falls down. I am standing on bodies.
A military barracks.
No bathroom. People stay still,
suffering their wounds.
People stay still. No bathroom.
A military barracks. I am standing on bodies,
fall down. Mainly babies and the elderly.
Everyone. The police begin firing.
When the Janjaweed come into the school,
children start jumping out windows.
The solution not military intervention.
The US keep its hands off Sudan, we demand
It's problematic to describe this as genocide.
I am paralysed. One after the other,
five of them. They stop their car
and throw him into a fire. Men
in uniforms with military insignia.
My son clings to my dress.
At eight o'clock in the morning I gather firewood.
It's problematic to describe this as genocide.
A bone field fifty metres by fifty.

*The non-italicised lines are quotations from eye-witness accounts from Darfur

Word From The Other Country

Where you've gone
    the air may be a Mardi Gras
of insects and pollen,
    but where I live
it's winter. World without ice cream,
    Amen.
I make do with soda bread,
    and spend long evenings
googling you. Most days,
    I know
it was nothing personal:
    I was the hobby
you took up to pass
    the worst years
of the recession. And when
    the sky comes down
I still rush out to take
    your favourite T-shirt
in out of the rain.

Shapeless Days Shuffling

Constant as stopped clocks or money
under the mattress. Your weak tea,
discoloured secrets and voice like snow through
a sulk black afternoon. The shapeless days shuffling
your serviceable drawers once more down the hallway,
like a minor character in one of Jane Austen's
lesser known novels. Until with its high pitched laugh
the universe signals not last minute Valentines
in big red envelopes—some cut-price Napoleon
in the end maybe taking you to the gates of Moscow—
but coming cobweb hair and rumours of cat-food:
the slow multiplication of all your small disappointments
into the bound volumes of broken promises
opening nightly now across the mahogany.

Retirement

The word you thought meant: time to tend the tulips
and perhaps, like your father, in later life develop
a big Dublin accent and definite knack of telling it
like it isn't; or summering by the seaside

where you'd employee as a manservant
a chimpanzee called Harold, and sometimes
leave your false teeth in the taxi after a weekend
corrupting young people in late night places

turns out to mean: sitting here (your eyes gone out
like candles) as the whiskey-voiced nurse reads aloud
from *The Daily Mirror*; and you remember

when life was something dreamt up at a bus-stop
on the outskirts of Athlone by a young fool
who thought the rain would stop soon.

from

Frightening New Furniture

(2010)

St. Stephen's Day, 1977

for my mother

Yesterday, in my new football boots I moved
like Kevin Keegan through the silver afternoon.
Today, *Mull of Kintyre* is number one
and the film director Howard Hawks is dead.
I take my football boots off,
am myself again.

You're still a skeleton with all day night sweats.
The doctor, who knows the why of everything
but this, has given you back for Christmas.
Most of the turkey goes leathery in the fridge.
Dad puts the telephone down, tells me
to extinguish the TV. The doctor
wants you back three days early.

Our Ford Cortina cradles you
through late afternoon streets,
all those lit windows and wreaths.
But we don't see them. And nothing is said
as we deposit you at Unit Seven,
Merlin Park Hospital. You at the door
giving a small pale wave. In the near distance
the disused boiler's giant chimney stack.
The rain saying terrible things
as we drive off, that Christmas
you didn't die.

That Was My Country

after Carol Ann Duffy

The phasing out of stone walls and saints.
The statues not daring to move.
When there was planning permission
for anything and morning
was breakfast baps and gravel
going back that road by the truckload.
When transparency meant
the skirts just kept getting shorter.
We so believed in sunshine,
on rainswept days we'd carry sunglasses
on top of our heads,
just in case. Wherever we wanted to go
Ryanair would get us almost
there and the world was
not our problem.

We still have butter
on our *Rich Tea* biscuits
for now, but no more
Coconut Creams;
and everywhere statues
of virgins and freedom fighters
think about stretching their legs.

Ourselves Again

In the park our ice lollies
fall victim to the June bank holiday heat,
while in glass rooms numbers moving
through dark computers
declare the future
finished.

Tomorrow, we'll have our double glazing
taken out; the crack put back
in the ceiling and a draught
installed under every door.
I'll attach a For Sale sign
to the seat of my pants.

Gangs of the angry unemployed
will bear down on the G Hotel
chanting "Down with *Daiquiris*
and *Slippery Nipples!* Give us back
our glasses of *Harp!*"

In pubs nationwide, the carpets of yesteryear
will be reinstated, and there'll be meetings
of Sinn Fein The Workers Party
going on permanently upstairs.

On our knees, we'll ask
for the unforgiveness of sins
and life not lasting.
We'll be ourselves again
and then some.

Without

The picture is brilliant and he's in it.
Townhouses and apartments with a marina.
He never lets anyone go without.

A hotel in the Black Sea resort of Varna.
A twenty thousand square foot spa.
The picture is brilliant and he's in it.

Dubai's largest tourist hostel.
One hundred and nineteen villas.
He never lets anyone go without.

He's pre-approved for everything.
Crowds helicopter in for his birthday.
The picture is brilliant and he's in it.

Headlines, when one morning before
breakfast he buys the island of Ireland.
He never lets anyone go without.

Combined anticipated sales: €500 million.
Developer's body found in shed.
The picture gone dark and him still in it.
He never let anyone go without.

March 5th, 2009

House Guest

after Elizabeth Bishop

For eighteen months
he's been staying
until the end of next week -
harder to pin down on any calendar
than the precise date of his world
uprising of the workers,
which he writes down for you nightly
on that day's anti-poll tax leaflet.

All the first week of January, fried slices
of the Christmas pudding his mother sent him
in the post are breakfast, lunch and dinner.
Work or the laundrette would get in the way
of his plans for the planet.
Your one bedroom flat is starting to smell.

When not away on a demo chanting
"Victory to Iraq!" his afternoons are spent
doing despicable things to worse women
in your bed. The pile of twenty pence pieces
on your bedside locker diminishes daily.

Yesterday, he was rushed to hospital
to have the y-fronts he's worn
for the past sixth months
surgically removed.

Today, he's what
emerges from your living room
sofa bed to tell you
where you're going wrong.

The Lost Years

Before I found the lesser poetry
of tax bills and unblocking the drains;
each Christmas Eve I was a pair
of disintegrated grey trousers, held
together by a socially concerned
safety pin. I'd emerge from the plane,
like a great historical event in the making,
with the ticket my mother sent me.

The rest of the year I was rumours
of sleeping bags on acquaintances' floors;
bounced cheques and borrowed fivers.
When challenged I was a suppressed sneer
at their small ideas and art of the probable.
I was the future they'd all one day wake up to;
and revolution meant more
than cheering on the bad guys
in *Die Hard* One, Two and Three.

Now, over breakfast I scour the Daily News
for oversized ideas and improbable tomorrows:
Students Waving Placards,
Whiskers For Slobadon Milosevic,
Anorexics Against Everything;
in daily instalments bequeath them
my rage at finding myself
lost to the lesser poetry
of tax bills and unblocking the drains;
nothing here to comfort me
but the complexity of an Israeli bomb
tearing a child's face off.

Days

We'd let the Daddy-long-legs take
the tower block hallway,
as we took time out
from demos in support
of those more fortunate
than ourselves
for a feast of taramosalata
on vintage brown bread
washed down
with the best can of *Kestrels*
a fifty pence piece could buy.

Our kitchen sink may have been
a failed utopian experiment;
the revolutionary group we'd just joined
a corpse passing wind.
But all we needed was
a draft to sit in
to talk about Agent Orange;
and with your rolled cigarettes,
my missing teeth,

we were insurgents waiting
to be hanged at dawn;
as we watched
the flat be torn apart
by a Keith Moon cat.
All dressed down
and someone to be.

Whatever happened to alienation?
Those were the days.

The Country I Dreamt Up While Protesting On Shop Street

Land without loneliness or weather.
Even the old men do not complain.
Yesterday my quick signature abolished poverty.
This morning my handshake ushered in
a new era of international happiness.
Women in provincial laundrettes wear
fantastic smiles. For their own good
schoolchildren are force fed my wife's
Complete History of Everything.
I can tolerate anything,
except being contradicted.
In the redesigned town square
rogue elements line up to confess.
It will be years yet before even a drunk dares
to stop and ask one of my statues a question.

Clear Out

Today it all goes to the dumpster,
my old political furniture:

the broken bookcase called
nationalisation of the banks;

the three legged dining chair called
critical support for the P.L.O;

the fringed, pink lampshade called
theory of the permanent revolution;

the collapsed sofa-bed called
excuses we made for Robert Mugabe;

the retired toilet seat called
the trade union movement.

And the man who spent
twenty five years sitting on it?

At three thirty six pm
in the stripped living room

I forget him. As of now
he never existed.

I'm too busy watching
the delivery man unload

frightening, new furniture
from that van pulled up outside.

June, 2007

Comrades

"As an ex-member of the Militant Tendency I wanted to bring down the State that most people supported. I'm glad the likes of me...were prevented from doing so... Thank you Special Branch."

Stephen Brent, Chichester, on the BBC website

1981. Capitalism was a Dimplex heater
with a broken switch. We'd
rush across the greasiest Formica,
the nastiest carpet to agree with each other
and cheer the news: *redundancies rocket,
stock markets on the floor.*

"Another Tory government
is out of the question," you told me.
It was February, 1982. The daffodils
couldn't have cared less.

"This puts a question mark over
Thatcher," I told you.
It was November, 1989. Hailstones
on Stoke Newington High Street.

Today, we meet with a history
of fried bread and picket lines
behind us. We believed in each other.
Now, it's a hundred years

since those afternoons
full of sunlight and clenched fists
when—in miners' strikes and poll tax riots—
we were like boys playing
in hoped for snow.

His Hour Come Round At Last

"What's the alternative?"

Condoleeza Rice

The Central Bank has declared a moratorium
on new sitting rooms and laughter, all relics
of the bygone bourgeois age known as
the week before last. The dog starts to hum
something by Woody Guthrie. These
are our *Grapes of Wrath* days. We'll
pack what we can into an old jalopie;
from now on live in a black and white
photograph by Dorothea Lange.
Tomorrow, we'll hang.

People will look at us in museums;
wonder what it was like
to be here, watching the guy
who's spent the past twenty years
turning himself on with pictures
of queues for government issue
Cup-a-Soup, blowing his nose
on other people's sleeves
reach for the alternative economic strategy
he keeps in an old Aldi bag;
when you'd rather anything
than live in a world where
he has a point.

Bookshop Romance

The girl behind the counter whispers: "Yes, Mother",
then puts the phone down with a cosmic sigh.
You look up from your D.H. Lawrence.
Something rustles in your corduroy trousers.

You want to shout: "Let me through!
I'm an existentialist"; to take her hand
and tell her: your own family Christmases
often resemble the aftermath of an embalming;
that your brother's a fully paid-up member
of *V-neck Sweaters for the Bomb*;
that most years you honour them
with your absence.

That you'd like her to come up
this evening to see your haiku
and the life you keep
in the shoebox under the bed.

That you've been admired
by women with bad judgment
all your life…

Midnight Mass

For one night only, everyone who's anyone
joins everyone who's not. His Worship, The Mayor,
thoughtfully scratches his left nostril, as the choir grapples
with *Jesus, Joy of Man's Desiring* by Johann Sebastian Bach.

Until the altos give way to an outbreak of shuffling feet,
a distant fit of coughing; and the Bishop steps forward:
"Our thoughts now turn to those who, during the past year,
have gone to that better place." For a moment the whole town
shuts its eyes. Mine stay open and focus on some of those
who've gone nowhere.

For whom my prescription, this time last year,
was *take carcinogens several times daily
and don't get back to me*; who by now should at least be
shuffling into their seats, like autopsies waiting to happen; or
sheepishly offering me the sign of peace
with big gangrenous hands;

who've turned up tonight looking absolutely fine,
when all year I've imagined worms having, for starters,
their right eyeballs before moving on to the main course
of brain.

Getting Somewhere

Turning forty two is like passing
through Portarlington on the train.
I will get somewhere eventually.

Today's paper says the everything
that was mine to win is now
the something I have to lose.

My daydreams busy
with clocks and budgets; I'm a man
destined to turn up early

for my own funeral, to spend
the morning redoing my tie
and wondering where the hell
everyone else has got to?

Together In The Future Tense

On a day that, for now, sits
unopened under the tree,
you'll push me uphill in a wheelchair;
say things like: *Augustus John,*
as you'll know, was obsessed
with motorcars and think
people know what you mean.

Every other Wednesday
we'll take the wrong medication
(you, mine and I, yours)
and the results will be
magnificent. I'll be forever answering
the question before last.

In our thoughts we'll commit
grotesque typographical errors:
for *Athens* read *Athenry*, for *Ralgex*
read *Canesten*, for *Disabled Toilet*
read *World Weightlifting Championships*,
for *Swan Lake* read *Loughrea*.

The once absolute monarchy
of my brain will grant autonomy
to my bits. Our bladders will be busy
writing their declarations of independence.

We'll be our very own festival of befuddlement;
as the light on the Aegean Sea
becomes a small boy
taking his ball home for the evening,
and the stray dogs wander off.

from

The Ghost In The Lobby

(2014)

Historically Sensible

You knew for a fact, they'd never
allow a pair of mad eyes with a pistol
near the Emperor and his wife;
and when they did, knew
the war would be done
before the Christmas tree went up
in Chichester town square;
and when it wasn't, that the Germans
must be forced to pick up the bill,
so they never did this again.
You knew for a fact, the Tsar
had a special place in the Russian peasant's heart;
and when he hadn't, that the Bolsheviks
wouldn't last five minutes.
And when they did, they were what
you'd been praying for all along.
Hitler was a joke with an Austrian accent
who'd never amount to anything,
and when he did, you knew for a fact
he had no interest in Warsaw, Kiev, Coventry.

You knew when the turbulence
had done its worst, the Shah
would still be sat on his Peacock throne,
looking taller than he actually was. Khomeni?
In five years' time no one
would remember his name.
And that cowboy actor was never
going to win the White House.

The hijackers you envisaged
always landed the plane
and let the passengers go.

On Getting Away With It

End of October. You go
coatless into a specially arranged
coincidence of sunlight.

I leave the house just
as the rain's begun taking itself
far too seriously.

You read mediocre poetry
to a different woman every
morning over breakfast.

My sex life is a door banging
in a house where
no one's lived for years.

Your greatest ambition
achieved; you're the most charismatic
TV repossession man in all

Hounslow; always
have the children thanking you
and laughing at your jokes

as you unplug and carry
Horrid Henry and *Scooby Doo*
down the driveway.

I'm the type who goes out to buy
a lawnmower
and comes back with an electric chair,

which I keep quiet
in the high weeds behind the garden shed,
spend the next ten years afraid

someone will make me
sit on it.

My Inner Conspiracy Theorist

Doesn't believe his own birth cert is genuine,
finds Charlie Sheen's most recent
speech from the balcony strangely
plausible; knows – the way all those Israelis knew
not to come into work that day – that swine flu
was manufactured in a laboratory funded
by Donald Rumsfeld, today's weather forecast
is a wicked lie, the dandelions exploding
up through his otherwise well kept lawn
were planted there by government agents
who lurk in the shrubbery at night,
that the Department of Agriculture laces
the sheep dip with weapons-grade
plutonium to hide the fact
he himself is actually
dead, assassinated years ago
by US special forces
during an otherwise enjoyable meal
in a Chinese restaurant
no one wants to talk about.

Remembering the Nineties

after Donald Davie

Our hair got smaller and the TV went on
forever. We waited
for The Stone Roses' second album, or watched
Party of Five. In Washington,
committees gathered to frown
at what had gone on in the President's trousers.

Northern Ireland paused for
what would eventually become
a fully formed thought. Rwanda
was a machete with names on it,
that sounded nothing like ours.
We protested French nuclear testing by
sampling South African white
wine's new found innocence.

Osama bin Laden was a rumour
no one believed and Saddam Hussein
an occasional burst of stomach acid
up the oesophagus. We could board planes
without anyone having to see us naked
through a machine first, and made our No
to apathy heard by not bothering to vote.

While we planned trips to places
we couldn't yet pronounce, politicians bickered
about the Romanians begging on Shop Street.

History was in the bathroom,
putting on her new face.

Not

You not here
to not know what
key goes in what lock;
to tell not exactly the truth
about who said what to whom;
to spend the whole first day
of the January sales
examining tea towels
you end up not buying; to notice
I've not yet mowed the lawn,
to not know when
the oil will run out, or have
a plan B, or a good word
for your enemies; to send me out
at four in the morning in search of
cigarettes; to stand smoking
by the kitchen window and say
this didn't happen; to smirk
and tell the world
moving furniture was never his thing
the day I do my shoulder in
carrying your coffin.

Them and You

after Dennis O'Driscoll

They go down to the house boat,
where someone is tuning an acoustic guitar.
You stay home alone in your tent.

They drive gleaming sports cars down
motorways built especially for them.
You stall on the Headford Road roundabout.

They are unruffled
as a table cloth at the Lord Mayor's banquet.
You turn an argument about punctuation into
a murder trial, yourself in the dock,
the judge putting on his black cap.

They get their names in the newspapers.
You count how many times
exactly.

They travel to watch Barcelona play
Real Madrid. Your team gets relegated.

They shake hands with people
you wish you'd been introduced to.

They know their way around the wine list.
You drink lager shandy because you're driving.

They have affairs with dental assistants
in third floor apartments by the docks.
You think of nothing else.

They can brush things off.
You have to know why
you weren't invited.

God Has Put You On Hold

And the world has no room
for the things you cannot forgive
in the hour of ropes and razorblades
the priest stuffs his suitcase

with things you cannot forgive.
All you have left are jokes blacker
than the priest stuffing his suitcase
as the water comes under the living room door

all you have left are jokes blacker
than having to rely on the generosity of the bankrupt
as the water comes under the living room door
you're a child playing with matches

and the generosity of the bankrupt.
In the hour of ropes and razorblades
you're a child playing with matches
and the world has no room.

Irish Government Minister Unveils Monument to Victims of Pro-Life Amendment

On a date to be confirmed,
when those who remember 1983
will sleep safely in their graves,
or be anxiously telling nurse
about the auld ones with crucifixes
they think are coming to get them

a girl, today
on holidays from primary school,
by then grown into
a Maggie Thatcher suit, will thank
the Chamber of Commerce
for use of their microphone
as a pulled chord unwraps
this thing chipped from stone

in memory
of those forced
to change trains at Crewe clutching
solitary suitcases that screamed
one night only,

those that bled out in the backs
of London taxis after journeys
made possible by post office accounts
and extra hours at the newsagent's;

all because of a stick
which, for them, turned
the wrong colour
the wrong year
in the wrong country.

And as the Minister continues,
across the road a little girl will grab
her mother's arm and ask:
what's that lady saying?

What The Virgin At Knock Would Say If She Could Speak

for Breda O'Brien and all at the Iona Institute

We need to get back
to when confirmed bachelors
found their own kind through holes in cubicles
during untelevised All Ireland Finals.
To when there were no government funded
lesbians on display in public parks,
or self-confessed sodomites in the Senate.
To when there was no obscene use for
Vaseline, or sexual intercourse in Headford.

To when no one put Coke bottles
where they weren't supposed to go.
And there were no automatic
washing machines for women to sit on
when Rock Hudson was unavailable.
To when the Irish people stood
at the end of lanes waiting
for nothing to happen,
which it mostly did.

To when young ones who forgot to cross
their legs at the crucial moment could be put
steam ironing curtains for the golf club, sheets
and pillowcases for your mother's B&B;
still be safely there eight o'clock
in the evening having hot flushes
the hottest day of that century
to which we must get back.

Austerity Mantra

Everything must be on the table.
Your ninety seven year old granny
        is no longer cost effective, would
benefit greatly from being brought face to face
        with a compassionate baseball bat.
The figures speak for themselves and will
        be worse by morning. The paraplegic
in his insanely expensive wheelchair
        will have to crawl as God intended.
Here are the figures that won't stop
        speaking for themselves, this is the table
everything must be on. Yesterday my name was
        Temporary Fiscal Adjustment.

Tonight, the insect in the radio calls me
        The Inevitable. When the economist
puts his hand up, take care not to cough.
        Everything's on the table and
the table's tiny. I'd send you a pillow
        to hold hard over the child's face
'til the kicking stops, but at current rates
        there'll be no pillow. I am the unthinkable
but you will think me. Pack her mouth
        with tea towels, hold down firmly
your old mildewed raincoat,
        'til there's no more breath.

Tomorrow I'll be known as
Four Year Consolidation Package.
        Lock the cat in the oven and bake
at two hundred degrees centigrade.
        Tie your last plastic bag over
your own head. The figures speak for themselves
        and there is no table.

Lament For A Latter Day Progressive

after Ernest Hemingway

When he visits his sister in Tucson
    and beholds
the magnitude of the burgers,
    he thinks it a pity
America was ever discovered;
    prefers nut roasts

done on a stove powered
    by fair trade
plutonium; invites
    an asylum seeker
to watch him eat breakfast
    every other Friday, asks himself
what this says about our society in which
    he insists on including you.

He takes pride in his work
    directing a non-profit
that makes socially aware
    pornography for
visually impaired former
    girl child soldiers. Before he left
his last wife, he had the affair
    with his secretary blessed
by a liberation theologist;

    last Saturday, spent
so long reading *The Irish Times*
    he grew a second
backside; emerged
    from the conservatory
emitting the words
    Polar Bears, Tibet,
Venezuela
    with the priestly whisper
of someone laying
    a wreath on his own grave.

Autobiography

I'm a ground floor room with a window
that will not close. I'm a cot
with a cloud of cigarette smoke
floating over it. I'm the watercress seeds
we planted at school today. I'm the week's
worth of ham sandwiches I left under the desk
last day before the summer holidays,
nineteen seventy seven. I'm one hundred
per cent in a science test once,
six percent in honours maths.
I'm the university degree I don't have.
I'm *Between The Wars* by Billy Bragg
for my eighteenth birthday and Auntie shrieking
over the fence, that I was conceived
out of wedlock. I'm action likely
to bring the Labour Party into disrepute.
I'm in contempt of court and must
apologise before we continue.
I'm fourteen cups of tea a day
most days (with the bag left in)
maybe ten cigarettes
in my whole life. I'm two weeks working
for *The Wall Street Journal.*
I'm yesterday's sausage roll
for breakfast today. I'm everything
I've been accused of
that wasn't true. I'm the things
they never found out about.

Mouth

When a whole cup of coffee goes screaming
into your beleaguered laptop or at
airport security you realise
you've mislaid your passport
and he spit-mutters:
you shouldn't have been born,
don't
take it personally.
He doesn't know
his own mouth. And when he tells you

he'd rather be fisted
by a fat trade unionist
than suffer another syllable
about your friend Mona's
most recent divorce/vaginal
dryness/pecuniary embarrassment;

tell him: *it can be arranged.*
And that, on occasions like
this, to talk with him is to wipe
the tenderest part of your arse
on the angriest nettles in his granny's
ever giving back garden.

You Can Take The Man Out Of Eyre Square But You Can't Take The Eyre Square Out Of The Man

for Susan

His head recognises the reality of *Supermacs*
but his heart still steals sweets from *Woolworths*.
His monologues are every St. Patrick's Day parade
since nineteen seventy four; his private thoughts
filthier than the old Eyre Square jax.

His political views are like Curran's Hotel,
not there anymore, but his words still subversive
as someone putting an orange jumpsuit
on Liam Mellows' statue.

His balances are healthier than the *Bank of Ireland*
and *Permanent TSB*, his mouth bigger
than *The Galway Advertiser*,
but his answer to everything is

Dunnes Stores. His stubble sometimes bristly
as a rough night in Richardson's;
his idea of himself inflated
as The Great Southern Hotel.

His greatest stroke of luck
drums and face painting
the day she stepped out of a car
and thought: 'I could live here'.

The Death of Baroness Thatcher

after Patricia McGuigan and Alexander Pope

Her hair was a headmistress dreaming
of again being allowed to use the cane.

Her ambition was a brass door knocker
on what was once a council house.

Her brain was a conversation about money
Sir Keith Joseph had with himself.

Her back passage was Basil Fawlty
complaining about car strikes to the Major.

The look in her eyes was a shoot to kill policy
in Northern Ireland.

Her sentimentality was a spinster's thimble
in which you could fit what's left of the Tory Party
in Scotland, Liverpool, Manchester,
Leeds, Sheffield, Newcastle...

Her clenched fist was a skinhead
in nothing but Union Jack y-fronts.

She said the word 'Europe'
like a woman coming down
from a severe overdose of Brussels Sprouts.

Her Christmases were dinner at Chequers
with a recently deceased sex offender.

Her 'out', 'no', 'never'
were striking print workers
being given the cat of nine tails.

Her fingers and thumbs
were ten riot shields in a row.

Her final nightmare
was the silent, black eyed ghosts
of Joe Green and David Jones,
who did nothing but each offer her
a hand.

David Gareth Jones, from Wakefield, died amid violent scenes outside Ollerton colliery in Nottinghamshire on 15 March 1984. On 15 June Joe Green was crushed to death by a lorry while picketing in Ferrybridge, West Yorkshire.

from

2016 –The Selected Satires of Kevin Higgins

(2016)

Blair's Advice

on hearing tell of his column in Sunday's Observer

Easy to say,
you'd rather make loud love
to Lord Prescott, or have
your face smashed between
Sir Cyril Smith's quivering cheeks
than read Tony Blair on how
the motorway to the mountaintop
he envisages lies
through the centre ground;
when you know neither
gentleman's available, right
here right now, to take you.

We need to make voting Labour pleasurable
for call centre managers and
estate agents of a certain age
as lowering their roasting
menopausal testicles
into a nice cold bath.

To this end, we need a leader
with ideas thrilling
as a dripping cistern,
a man (or woman) likely conceived during
a Conservative Association dinner
somewhere in darkest Buckinghamshire;

who, while his or her fellow students
were thoughtlessly dancing the blues,
bravely danced the beige;
a person of exemplary character apart
from that one conviction for stealing
the brass handles off
their own father's coffin.

We must offer hope
to those who aspire to shop
for gourmet sausage meat
at Waitrose, and not
waste time on people who perspire
as they rifle through packets
of past-their-use-by-date
picnic ham at Aldi.

17/5/15

Irish Air: Message from the CEO

with thanks to Padraig McCormack for the inspiration

Every day under the sky
in this teeny weeny country
they think belongs to them,
people kick football, jog
up and down promenades;
run red faced for buses
on wet mornings; days off they climb
hyperventilating briefly
up shaky looking ladders;
they drive miles through countryside
to attend funerals of people
they never met, and roll
car windows down. They give
others who've collapsed gasping
in the street
amateur mouth to mouth.
When everyone else is out,
they make obscene phone calls,
pant down lines at women
they think live alone.
Come the six o'clock bell,
those not trapped in traffic
or enrolled in evening classes,
slob on a bewildering variety of sofas,
play until bedtime with remotes.
All the time taking for granted
the luxury: breath

which, given the cost, we can no longer offer
free. Much as we all enjoy
breathing, our current funding model
is no longer sustainable.

Every country in the OECD,
	excepting Ireland, levies
a small charge for breath.
	Air is important.
We must stop disrespecting it
	by failing to give it a price.

As of October, *Irish Air*
	will begin attaching meters
to the side of each adult's skull.
	No eighteenth birthday party
will be complete without a visit from us.
	It will be an offence,
punishable by a law made up yesterday,
	to tamper with, or remove,
your personal meter.
	There are no exemptions
for the disabled, the elderly, or the insane.
	Air will still be available free
to children and the deceased.
	When you smother your spouse,
inform us here at *Irish Air*,
	and we'll reduce your bill
by the appropriate amount.
	The cranium of every tourist
will be fitted with a temporary meter,
	to be removed only on their exit
from the country. Those whose bills
	remain unredeemed will not be allowed
leave. Diplomats are exempted.

	Resisters will have their air flow
reduced to the occasional puff,
	every half hour or so.
If you have reason to believe
	your personal air flow

has been erroneously reduced,
    call our office
and speak to one of our staff.
    It is an offence
to tamper with, remove, or shove
    your personal meter
anywhere obscene.
    Our arses are important to us
and we will not tolerate them
    being interfered with
by citizens of this teeny weeny country
    you think belongs to you.

Irish Liberal Foresees Own Enduring Relevance

My words are smoother than the essential oils
the Taoiseach last week
had his parliamentary assistant rub
into his badly traumatised buttocks.
My psychotherapist insists
half the people who've taken
shotguns to their own heads
during this recession would've reconsidered,
if only they'd heard me talk for an hour
each week about the dangers of Sinn Féin,
or how I live in the hope of a woman Pope.

I'm all for the good people of middle Ireland
making their point in a dignified manner
with china cups of nothing stronger than tea in their hands.
But when thugs from the far parts start burning vans
and generally acting as if they owned the place;
and gurriers from the depths begin picking up bricks
and tossing words so terrible
they're not even in the dictionary
at the Minister for Poverty's hair-style.
(How would you like your wife,
sister, great grandmother,
kidnapped in her car
for two and a half hours?)

The world will not be changed by fools
banging on the bonnet of a BMW.
But by the likes of me talking
against social exclusion in TV studios.
And fundraising concerts organised
by former pop-stars.
And the well-meaning priest
with whom I regularly have dinner;

between the two us we've enough
concern for the poor to construct a second
Fergal Keane of the BBC,
as a back-up in case
the existing one breaks.

Trust in us. Pay no heed
to the sweary-mouthed crowd,
who if they're not put back where they belong
will soon be eating pot noodle from scooped out skulls
confiscated from their betters
in defiance of international law.
By the likes of them,
the world must not be changed.

Renewable Energy: Cora Sherlock's Excellent Suggestion

"Over 15,500 human remains incinerated to heat UK hospitals over 2-year-period. http://www.telegraph.co.uk/health/healthnews/ 10717566/Aborted-babies-incinerated-to-heat-UK-hospitals.html #800babies #outrage @amnesty" Tweet by Cora Sherlock of the Pro-Life Campaign

We must stop giving it away for nothing
—our greatest natural resource —
the Department of Finance estimates
Tallaght Hospital could heat itself
entirely on foetuses properly burnt
in one of those state of the art
energy efficient furnaces that are
all the rage in Sweden.

Within the lifetime of this government
every hospital in the country could be fuelled
by the unwanted contents of visiting wombs.
The minority of cranks aside,
the average foetus would be delighted
to make this small contribution towards
society's continued warmth.

And when the ban on contraceptive devices
is re-introduced; every last diaphragm,
IUD, cock-ring, and bit of rubber
ribbed for your pleasure incinerated
in a field outside Ballinspittle,
after a blessing by Mother Teresa,
(specially flown in from
the black beyond)
and the conception rate soars
back towards

the traditional twelve
pregnancies per lifetime, two thirds,
we estimate, resulting in terminations,
we can start talking
about the export market.

Economists say the uteruses
of the greater Dublin area alone
could light the living rooms
of a medium sized British city,
such as Bradford.

Education is key.
To get the lady parts of the country
conceiving as they'll have to,
every pubescent girl,
on her fifteenth birthday,
will be shown her way around
the first twenty pages of the Kama Sutra
by a fully qualified curate
under the age of seventy.

This policy's success
will abolish talk of deficits
and oil prices. Instead,
we'll debate furiously
whether to blow our vast surplus
on a few thousand more
unemployed tin whistle players
with the hint of an English accent,
or free nose jobs and tummy tucks
for the wives of the wealthy—the biggest
plastic surgery project in world history
since NASA's unsuccessful attempt
to build another Joan Rivers.

The Islamisation of Birmingham

*"there are actual cities like Birmingham that are totally Muslim
where non-Moslems just simply don't go"*

Steve Emerson, Terrorism Expert, on Fox News

Most reckon it was the day Ozzy Osbourne
walked out the gates of Winson Green Prison,
ready to commit acts of musical terrorism
in a desperate effort to undermine Christ,
that the City began turning instead
to Mecca. All agree

the situation grew
more serious each time Roy Wood sang:
I Wish It Could Be Christmas Everyday
in the hope we wouldn't notice
the big mad beard he got
at a training camp in Pakistan.

Spaghetti Junction was already
jammed with Moslem only vehicles,
the night the Mulberry Bush
and Tavern in the Town
were blown up by Moslems
disguised as IRA men.
Since then every nil all draw
between Aston Villa and Birmingham City
has been celebrated by stadiums half full
of nothing but Moslems.

Truth is, it started way back,
the night Chamberlain signed
his secret treaty with Adolf, agreeing
in the event of war with Russia, to hand
the birthplace of Enoch Powell
over to the Islams.

These days the local economy is mostly
Jaguar Cars and Cadbury's chocolate
being secretly manufactured by Moslems
for export to terrorist countries busy
thinking up new ways to kill us.

from

The Minister for Poetry Has Decreed

(2016)

The Art of Political Rhetoric

I am glad you asked me that question
(and not the other one). Absolutely.
Under no circumstances,
except those that will definitely arise.
We need to have a conversation;
and offer the public big solutions
to problems they didn't know they had.
We must build an economy based
on real people going
backwards up the escalator
towards a future in which
they can all equally
disbelieve. The inquiry into these
matters must have teeth
or, at least, dentures.
We will make this country a hub
for inward upvestment from
the Apples, the Googles,
the Redtubes. It's a zero-sum
game between Limerick
and Drogheda United in which
neither team will turn up,
if they know what's good for them.
Hardly anyone will die
because of what we propose. We will provide
the twenty first century hospitals
the squeezed muddle have been roaring
and shouting for. We are committed,
absolutely, to exclusivity in the arts.
Ballet dancing for big people. That sort of thing.
We will fill the country
with so many green-house gasses,
it will float off, of its own volition,
into the sky.
I was privileged to attend yesterday
the least important meeting

in the history of the world.
This is not a time for soundbites,
but I can feel
what I sincerely hope
is the hand of posterity
up my derriere
and think it might be stuck there.

Against Plan to Ruin Revolution Day with Strike

for the Luas workers

We're all for workers' rights,
like nothing more
than to browse the better variety
of coffee table book for poignant
photographs: cloth caps and blue overalls
whose existences were
exquisitely terrible, down to the way
typhus so cinematically throttled
their two, three, four, and five
year olds, same day industrial slicers
took their little fingers, or perhaps,
if they were lucky,
a thumb.

Because of those bastard
trade unions, we shall not
see their picturesque likes again.
But what makes our pulsing
haemorrhoids pop is Dublin
tram workers' ongoing plan
to make their customers walk, to disrupt
Revolution Day celebrations
by going on strike for money
they wouldn't know what to do with
if they had it.

The men and women of 1916
didn't go out that day
so that a hundred years later
tourists could be inconvenienced,
and distinguished men in eco-friendly
cashmere sweaters made irritable
in their magnificent armchairs.

When, come that Monday,
the ghosts of Markievicz, Connolly, & Pearse
alight at Heuston Station; they must
be allowed go about the business
of watching us pretend to remember them,
unencumbered by picket lines,
or small people daring
to take their share.

Ghost of Health Service Future

Back when we had only
the occasional old five pound note
invested under our long suffering mattresses,
in the golden age of scurvy, typhus, plague
there was always something fatal
to take the frail off our hands
at hardly any expense to anyone,
bar the price of digging the grave.

Now, some scientist comes flapping daily
from the laboratory to declare another bastard
disease sadly no longer incurable.
The long term cost of all this
getting better will be our ruin.

The future we offer you will be short
and affordable.

For starters, every cup of tea will be tested
to ensure it contains appropriate levels
of the deadlier strains of E-Coli.
Those suffering from cardiac
arrhythmia or elevated blood pressure
will be taken off all expensive medication,
and shouted at three hours a day
by unemployable sociopaths,
so happy at the hint of a job,
they'll work for nothing.

From his or her fortieth birthday onwards
asthmatics, and those with chronic
bronchitis, sarcoidosis, and cystic fibrosis
will receive no treatment at all,
unless they agree to immediately
take up smoking.

Those with Crohn's disease, IBS,
or colitis will be force fed three loaves
of slightly stale bread
until they stop complaining.

Everyone availing of our public health system
will be subject to random spot checks
on their way to work, to make sure
they've gobbled their daily ration
of fat only yoghurt.

Schoolteachers will be empowered
to wire children judged too thin
up to the school sugar pump,
until they have expanded sufficiently.

Those who, despite all this,
insist on turning seventy five
will be tickled to death with feather dusters,
they will be expected to supply themselves;
their laughing corpses dumped
in the nearest river to further
infect the water supply.

Over the next five years,
we will replace the costly chaos
of our hospital system with the eternal calm
of the graveyard.

A Day of Just Yes

Word is:

the system of storms
building mid-Atlantic has now
obligingly cancelled itself out;

all remaining car accidents
have been put off until tomorrow;

no further bankruptcy notices
will come into existence
until at least Monday,
as there's no one home
to open the envelopes;

the shadow on your mother's
right lung will not be detectable
on an x-ray until next Wednesday
week at the earliest;

elected representatives
are permitted, for one day only,
to walk the streets openly
shaking peoples' hands
without anyone wanting
to lock them in the boot
of an ancient Ford Escort
to think about what they've done
and what they've failed to do;

commentators from across
the ideological spectrum agree,
even Auntie Bridie's sciatica
is better than it was
this time last week;

the other side's slogans are,
this morning, flags
madly cheering
your victory;

the rooftop crows for once
maintain a dignified silence
and appear to be enjoying
this sunshine,
which the old lady in the paper shop
says is promised
to last.

23-5-15

Exit

for Darrell Kavanagh in his hour of need

There will be no more thunderstorms
sent across the Channel by the French,
no acid rain floating in from Belgium.
Pizza Hut will offer a choice of
Yorkshire Pudding or Yorkshire Pudding.

You'll spend the next twenty seven bank holidays
dismantling everything you ever bought from IKEA.
The electric shower your plumber,
Pavel, put in last week will be taken out
and you'll be given the number of a bloke
who's pure Billericay. Those used to caviar
will have jellied eels forced
down their magnificent throats.
Every fish and chip shop
on the Costa del Sol will in time
be relocated to Ramsgate or Carlisle.

All paving stones laid by the Irish
will be torn up to make work
for blokes who've been on the sick
since nineteen seventy six.
Those alleged to be involved in secretly
making spaghetti bolognaise
will be arrested and held
in a detention centre near Dover. Sausage dogs
will be put in rubber dinghies
and pointed in the general direction
of the Fatherland. Neatly sliced
French sticks topped with Pâté
will make way for fried bread
lathered with Marmite.

There'll be no more of those new
names for coffee your gran
can't pronounce. The entire royal family
will be shipped back to Bavaria, with the exception
of the Duke of Edinburgh who'll be given
a one way ticket to Athens. Curry
will no longer by compulsory
after every twelfth pint of Stella,
which itself will only be available
by special permission of the Foreign Office.

We'll give India back its tea, sit around increasingly
bellicose campfires in our rusting iron helmets,
our tankards overflowing with traditional Norse mead.

Afterword

by Philip Coleman

In the closing lines of the poem entitled 'Selfie' in the opening section of this volume, Kevin Higgins writes:

> The crack down the gable wall
> has moved and is now
> within me.

The poet is not having the *craic* with his readers here, no matter how much laughter this and other poems in *Song of Songs 2.0* may provoke in performance. On the contrary, this poem, like many others by Kevin Higgins, is less concerned with comedy than it is with exposing the ultimately banal but ubiquitous presence of tragedy in modern life. 'The truth is that no definition of tragedy more elaborate than "very sad" has ever worked,' Terry Eagleton suggested in his book *Sweet Violence: The Idea of the Tragic* (2002). The idea provides an interesting key to unlocking what lies at the heart of Kevin Higgins's very sad – if also, often, horribly funny – poems. They are tragic in the sense that they expose the profound and grotesque sadness of our current historical predicament. The poems that open this volume cast the caustic comedies of Kevin Higgins's earlier poems in a new light – demanding that we read the poet's work in a way that recognises the social, political and historical challenges out of which it has emerged – but also inviting us to think about what role poetry might play as we contemplate our 'post-truth', 'fake news' futures.

Writing in *The Cambridge Introduction to Irish Poetry, 1800-2000* (2008), Justin Quinn described Kevin Higgins as a poet whose work contains 'a social critique as lithe and imaginative as that of the con-merchants who run the show.' The comparison is illuminating, not least because it suggests that the forms of expression and imagination engaged in and by Higgins's early poems embody all the cunning and deviousness of language as it has been manipulated by his many targets. In the poem entitled 'To certain lyric poets', from his first collection *The Boy With No Face* (2005), Higgins wrote of a 'lyric poet [who] sees / his own reflection everywhere':

> He's been known
> to agonise for hours
> over a single word
> and each one of them
> is precisely meant
> because, to him,
> words are beautiful things,
> flowers to be arranged
> around the altar of his ego.

These lines illustrate some of the strategies the speaker seeks to criticise in the 'certain lyric poets' of the title. As an exercise in satire, however, the poem succeeds in part because it is informed by the very methods and modes of expression that it would claim to dismantle. In a sense, the poem works because Higgins wears the mask of the self critiqued in it. In the same way that Jonathan Swift assumed the voice of power in his great works of satire – think of the devastating act of ideological mimicry that is *A Modest Proposal* – Higgins's poems often proceed through and by acts of powerful and unsettling ventriloquism, performing his own identities and the identities of others with searing self-laceration.

In the title-piece of his prose collection *Poetry, Politics and Dorothy Gone Horribly Astray*, written in 2004, Higgins wrote:

Almost every poet I know is prone to exaggerate the influence poetry can exert on world events. Maybe it's the cold reality of poetry's marginal position in society which leads many of us, particularly at a time of crisis [...] to talk in loud excited voices about how poetry can supposedly make politicians sit up and listen or even 'change the world'. This benign egocentricity is perhaps a necessary indulgence to save us from vanishing entirely into our garrets, or academia, convinced of the total irrelevance of what we do.

In the course of his essay, however, Higgins argues that the best thing writers can do is 'bear witness as honestly and as well as [they] possibly can', not just to the hypocrisy of particular individuals, but also to the broader international crises of our time – from the so-called 'War on Terror' to what he has described as the degeneration of 'the high Socialist hopes of the early twentieth century ... into ... sordid everyday tyranny' in an essay on Albanian poet Visar Zhiti. In his piece on Zhiti, also collected in *Poetry, Politics and Dorothy Gone Horribly Astray*, Higgins is not afraid to disagree with 'socialist friends' who have criticised the works of certain poets because of their perceived detachment from the world of politics and economic materiality. Unlike those who would 'act Stalin when dealing with poetry which doesn't appear to serve the cause', as he puts it in the same piece, Higgins is a poet whose work credits the value of poetry for its ability to raise consciousness and conscience in the public sphere. For Higgins, poetry is always a public event, and he has steadily insisted on the place of the poet in the life of the state over the course of a career that is amply represented throughout the pages of *Song of Songs 2.0: New & Selected Poems*. This is reflected in his work on the performance poetry circuit, certainly, but it also has to do with his sense of the social and public potency of the word on the page as it merges with the reader's consciousness.

Kevin Higgins's contribution to the development of Irish satire is indisputable, but his work also engages with the private sphere. He is a lyric poet, but he is one for whom the pressures of the public world are too great, and too serious, to ignore. The poem 'Clear Out', from *Frightening New Furniture* (2010), explores the relationship between domestic or personal space and the public world of politics in its imagery and language:

> Today it all goes to the dumpster,
> my old political furniture:
> the broken bookcase called
> nationalisation of the banks;
> the three legged dining chair called
> critical support for the P.L.O;
> the fringed, pink lampshade called
> theory of the permanent revolution....

Higgins's work explores on many levels the application of political and social theory to daily lived experience – it is no accident that his work is suffused with references and allusions to the many writers and readers he has read, from Leon Trotsky and Philip Larkin to Dennis O'Driscoll and Stevie Smith – but it is also direct in its evaluation of the usefulness or otherwise of theoretical and artistic speculation. As he puts it in 'A Balancing Act', from *The Boy With No Face* (a poem not included here but well worth seeking out, like many other poems that did not make the final cut for this selection):

> You who've come to understand
> dialectical materialism like the back of your hand:
> your ideas as clinical as surgical instruments:
> must know knowledge is a commodity
> all too often squandered, that the trick
> is not to spot the flaw in every fabric;
> to conduct elaborate experiments
> in new forms of paralysis.

Higgins wears his learning lightly, as did Patrick Kavanagh. Like Kavanagh, indeed, Higgins does not take himself too seriously – but seriously enough that his poems affirm the value of intelligent, informed and passionate artistic engagement with the world at every turning.

Song of Songs 2.0 gathers work from each of Higgins's published volumes to date, including the pamphlets *The Ministry for Poetry Has Decreed* (Culture Matters, 2016) and *The Selected Satires of Kevin Higgins* (Nuascéalta, 2016). The 'original' *Song of Songs* is known by various titles, in several languages, and it is found in the holy texts of both Christianity and Judaism. It is tempting to say that *Song of Songs 2.0* is a twenty-first century secular take on a spiritual classic. The poem 'Song of Songs 2.0' certainly sends up the ancient piece, in a way, and it is full of images that will be read, and heard, as instances of Higgins's searing and dark poetic comedy in performance:

> How glorious your feet stuffed into trainers
> Oh lavatory attendant's daughter....

But what are we laughing at as we laugh at this poem if not ourselves and the world we have learned to destroy while we claim to cherish it? Towards the end of the poem the speaker says:

> Let us get up early to the canal
> by the chemical weapons factory
> and see what dies there.

This is an invitation to view the world in all of its contemporary decay, where the solace of religious or, indeed, secular, succour are no longer possible to attain – not that they ever were. What is attainable, however, out of the bleakness of this vision, is a new, more honest and more humane, form of understanding that surpasses the surfaces of satire as mere entertainment.

Kevin Higgins, as a master satirist, knows that his work must and does aim, finally, towards some form of positive social transformation. As he puts it in 'Poetry, Politics and Dorothy Gone Horribly Astray':

If we don't at least convince ourselves that poetry can matter, then how on earth can we expect to convince anyone else? The truth is poetry can sometimes play a role in actually challenging people's minds, by convincing the reader (or listener) emotionally of an idea to which he or she may be intellectually opposed. If a poem can win the ideologically hostile reader's heart, then his or her head will surely follow. Such a heightened experience of poetry can lead to a transformed world view for the reader.

Song of Songs 2.0 presents the reader with arresting and often disturbing representations of the self and the world on almost every page, but its greatest achievement may be in forcing us to think again about what poetry is capable of doing, what it is for, and what role it may have in helping us to negotiate the terrifying times that lie ahead. In the words of the Albanian poet Visar Zhiti, acknowledged and admired as a major figure by Higgins:

> And, still, I write poems
> Though no one reads them.
> Perhaps the wind does not read the stars at night,
> Maybe the cliffs at the seaside
> Feel nothing of the fury of the waves.

'The Epilogue (Of Which Time Makes a Preface)'

If you have not read Kevin Higgins's poems, now, more than ever, may be the time to read them. *Song of Songs 2.0* provides a brilliant, timely introduction.

March 2017

Philip Coleman teaches in the School of English, Trinity College Dublin.

Sections of this essay were first published under the title '"Against the Iron Railings of History": the Poetry, and some of the Prose, of Kevin Higgins' in the *Irish Left Review* (August 2011).

KEVIN HIGGINS is co-organiser of Over The Edge literary events in Galway, Ireland. He teaches poetry workshops at Galway Arts Centre, Creative Writing at Galway Technical Institute, and is Creative Writing Director for the NUI Galway Summer School. He is poetry critic of *The Galway Advertiser*. Kevin has published four collections of poetry with Salmon, *The Ghost In The Lobby* (2014), *Frightening New Furniture* (2010), *Time Gentlemen, Please* (2008), and his best-selling first collection, *The Boy With No Face* (2005), which was shortlisted for the 2006 Strong Award for Best First Collection by an Irish poet. His poetry is discussed in *The Cambridge Introduction to Modern Irish Poetry* and features in the generation defining anthology *Identity Parade —New British and Irish Poets* (Ed. Roddy Lumsden, Bloodaxe, 2010) and in *The Hundred Years' War: modern war poems* (Ed. Neil Astley, Bloodaxe, April 2014). A collection of Kevin's essays and book reviews, *Mentioning The War*, was published by Salmon Poetry in 2012. Kevin's poetry has been translated into Greek, Spanish, Italian, Japanese, Russian, & Portuguese. In 2014 Kevin's poetry was the subject of a paper 'The Case of Kevin Higgins,' or, 'The Present State of Irish Poetic Satire' presented by David Wheatley at a Symposium on Satire at the University of Aberdeen. He was Satirist-in-Residence at the Bogman's Cannon (2015-16). *2016 - The Selected Satires of Kevin Higgins* was published by NuaScéalta in early 2016. A pamphlet of Kevin's political poems *The Minister For Poetry Has Decreed* was published in December by the Culture Matters imprint of the UK based Manifesto Press. His poems have been praised by, among others, Tony Blair's biographer John Rentoul, Observer columnist Nick Cohen, and Sunday Independent columnist Gene Kerrigan; and have been quoted in *The Daily Telegraph*, *The Times* (UK), *The Independent*, and *The Daily Mirror*. *The Stinging Fly* magazine recently described Kevin as "likely the most read living poet in Ireland."